Beautiful Ben – My Son with Autism

Our family stories of life with Ben

Sue Lehr

Book design: Michelle Cryan

Printed by Vicks Lithograph and Printing
Yorkville, NY

First printing: August 2009

LIBRARY OF CONGRESS CONTROL NUMBER: 2009907619
Lehr, Sue
Beautiful Ben – my son with autism/Sue Lehr

www.beautifulben.com

ISBN 978-0-615-30747-3

For Robert
Because I love you

For Ben
My Beautiful Son who has taught me so much

For all the people who helped us along the way

And for all the parents of children with disabilities who continue
to struggle and who have their own stories to tell

Table of Contents

Beautiful Ben – My Son with Autism

Introduction – Our Family Stories

By Sue Lehr

This book is about my adopted biracial son Ben who is almost 36 years old now. His autism was diagnosed in 1978 when he was four. He was a complex and complicated child, but we learned how to accommodate and adjust, but others did not. When he was in high school he learned to communicate with us using facilitated communication, a form of assisted typing. Our story begins with one of Ben's typed homework assignments for a high school class. It is a metaphor for our life with him.

A bit of background

Early in our marriage, Bob and I had decided to adopt "hard to place" racially mixed children. When we met in 1961, and as we learned about each other and life in general, the times were turbulent. The civil rights movement, the Vietnam war, the assassinations of President Kennedy and Bobby Kennedy, and later Martin Luther King, the feminist revolution and what we were learning in our college courses unsettled our beliefs and compelled us think for ourselves, challenge what we believed, and reconstruct new ideas about ourselves, our future, and the world we were coming to know. Bob and I became social activists marching against the war, speaking out for peace, challenging racism, and joining politically active groups. Indeed, we questioned everything. We spent hours talking with each other. These discussions enervated us. On a more personal level we were trying to figure out how we could change the world into a better, kinder, gentler place for all people. What governed us most was The Golden Rule – treat others as you would want to be treated.

Our first child, Sherry, was born in 1968, but it was almost five years later when we adopted Penny. She was four months old, born to teenage parents. Her mother was African American and Native American. Her father was Irish. Ben was our second "hard to place" adoption. He was just five months old when he joined our family. As an infant and toddler he seemed to fit right into our happy family, but it wasn't long before we began to notice things that made us wonder if he was okay. His eyesight was compromised by what we thought was a "lazy eye"; one eye that turned inward toward his nose. Our pediatrician assured us Ben would outgrow this and be fine. As a toddler he was part of a child development class at the college where my husband taught. The third and fourth graders studied his development and plotted his progress with walking and talking and play. They loved Ben's weekly visits and he seemed to relish the chaotic attention. No one raised any concerns. We thought he was "normal".

We did take him to an ophthalmologist when his eye did not seem to improve, but it was a devastating experience. One which caused us to take a new and more rational look at Ben's development. Eventually, a different eye doctor prescribed glasses to correct his vision problems, but Ben was certainly not a cooperative "four eyes". He persisted in taking off his glasses and just dropping them. We constantly were finding them and perching the glasses back on his broad nose. Over time, his eyes did seem to improve.

When Ben was three years old, we enrolled him in a preschool program for "handicapped children only." By then, we recognized that his development was not normal in some ways. He could walk, but his gait was awkward. He could pick up things like toys, but he didn't play with them. He rarely spoke any real words, instead making nonsensical sounds that seemed to amuse him. Socially, he was aloof. He didn't shy away from others, he just showed no interest in them. He didn't seek attention, but was content to play in his own way; later we would say, "in his own little world".

Ben was a little over four years old in 1978 when he was officially diagnosed with Classical Autism. Getting to this diagnosis was not easy, but it enabled us to foresee some of the problems that lay ahead, or so we thought. His two years in a segregated preschool forced us to recognize his limitations, but also caused us to seriously consider what his future should be. Bob and I agreed that we didn't want his life to be defined by his autism. We wanted him to have all the same opportunities as "non-handicapped" children. Because of our experiences with Ben's two older sisters, we learned what his life could be like, but we began to recognize that we would have to be very thoughtful, tenacious, and perseverant in pursuing this. Little did we realize that it would be much, much harder than we expected. There were so many things that we never anticipated.

We moved to a new community, partly so that Ben could attend a school where he would be in classrooms along with non-handicapped peers. This school, named Jowonio (an Native American Indian word meaning "to set free"), based its practices on the belief that all children would benefit from learning together. The administrators and staff expected their students to become real citizens in a complex society where everyone is valued for what they are able to contribute. Jowonio rejected the "deficit" model of handicapism that asserted that children like Ben needed to be re-mediated or fixed before they could attempt to enter society. Bob and I loved this enriching life for Ben and us, and we naively believed that everything would be fine now.

Our new home sat on the edge of a small lake in a rural part of upstate New York. Our neighbors welcomed us and Ben became part of the neighborhood kids. He attended birthday parties, played with the kids on the street, and began developing friendships. For the two years that Ben attended Jowonio it was a very happy time for all of us.

From the time Bob and I first met, we have loved to travel and explore the country. Having three children didn't deter us from taking long camping trips exploring the United States and eventually Europe. Ben loved these trips. He even learned how to be potty trained on one of them. This was really a challenge, but quite fun too. In a way, it was a metaphor for the risks and challenges that we knew we would face as Ben became older. Bob and I talked long and hard about what was the best thing for Ben to enable him to be successful, without taking anything away from our other two children. We wanted them to love their brother, not feel sorry or embarrassed by him. We enlisted their help in making experiences for Ben fun and educational. We relied on them to be his peer models and they were great. They celebrated his successes and were proud of his accomplishments. They never doubted him.

Over these years, Bob and I became involved in a number of professional organizations such as the ARC and local human service agencies that served people with disabilities. Initially, Bob served on several boards of directors for local organizations, but was quickly elevated to state offices. In the late 1970's he was appointed by then New York Governor Mario Cuomo to the Board of Visitors for our local developmental center, a large bed residential institution for children and adults with mental retardation and other developmental disabilities. As a board member, Bob was expected to visit the "center" frequently to oversee the administration and care of its residents. We both were familiar with these types of facilities, but now we saw them with new clarity. This was not where Ben was going to live, ever. We didn't know where he would eventually live, but we also realized that he would move on some day. We would not live forever, and we didn't want Ben to be so dependent upon us that he could not survive without us. As we engaged with other parents and families who were members of these same organizations, we cringed when we saw adults with disabilities being led hand-in-hand by their aging parents. We vowed that would not be what would happen for Ben. We also vowed that we would not expect our daughters to be his caregivers forever. We didn't know how we would do it, but we committed ourselves to assuring that Ben would be able to live an independent life with whatever help he needed to be safe and free. To make this a reality, however, Bob and I, along with our daughters, began to identify what Ben needed in order to succeed.

One of the first things we intuitively knew was that he needed to be among friends his own age, and he needed to have the same kinds of experiences as common ground. He went trick-or-treating every year. He participated in neighborhood activities along with the neighborhood kids. They taught him to "hang out" and even pushed Bob and I to let him try new things, to take risks they felt he could handle. Yes, we were scared of what might happen, but we firmly believed that if Ben had real friends who saw beyond his autistic quirks, he would be okay. It was extremely difficult for us, but we began to step back and let his sisters and friends support him.

While all these positive things were happening, however, Ben graduated from Jowonio and entered our local elementary school. Their philosophy was dramatically different from that of Jowonio's and it wasn't long before we were clashing. They were unprepared for the complexities that Ben presented, and the administrators seemed unable to commit to helping the staff with training and support. The teachers tried, at least in the beginning, but it didn't last. They were schooled in the segregated deficit model of special education while Bob and I were dedicated to the belief that Ben should be fully included in the regular classroom along side his peers. Reluctantly, we finally "duked it out" in a lengthy and painful due process hearing. In a legal process like this, no one wins. The only point on which everyone agreed was that Ben could not remain in this school. The hearing officer's final decision placed Ben in a neighboring urban school district in their new "Integrated Autistic Program" modeled upon Jowonio's. We were hopeful that things would improve for Ben, but we also knew there were going to be hurdles and rough spots. There were, and then some, but Ben also had some wonderful experiences in his new school.

I enrolled in a Ph.D. program in Special Education at Syracuse University. I had been working as an administrator of a program for adults with disabilities at a local community college. My experiences here and with Ben made me realize I needed to learn more. Eventually, I worked on a project that brought me into contact with parents all over the country who had children with disabilities. While in graduate school I also worked at the Facilitated Communication Institute at Syracuse

University which brought me into contact with many more families and individuals with disabilities.

Ben remained in the "Integrated Autistic Program" in the Syracuse City School District until he graduated in 1992. It was during this time that Ben learned how to use facilitated communication and was given the homework assignment that will introduce this book. He joined after school clubs, wrote a column in the high school newspaper, attended the senior prom, and walked the stage at graduation. We were so proud of him.

Although we all were excited that Ben had graduated, we fully understood that his life now would be even more complicated. How would he spend his time? What would he do? His friends went on to college or joined the military. He became isolated and lonely. Bob's father had moved in with us after suffering a debilitating stroke. He and Ben just did not get along. Life at home was tense to say the least. I was trying to work full time, write my Ph.D. dissertation, and maintain a reasonable family life when Ben announced he wanted to move out. I thought it was because of the conflicts with Grandad, but later I learned Ben wanted to move out for his own reasons. We have always honored what Ben wanted and so we began the process of figuring out what this might look like.

It took time, money, and many stressful minutes, but eventually Bob and I bought a house for Ben. It was in the neighborhood where Ben had gone to school and was close to one of his former teachers who promised to look out for him. With Ben taking the lead, we advertised for housemates. Around Labor Day of 1995 Ben moved into his new home with two young men as his housemates. Neither of these fellows had ever met anyone with autism, but they agreed to give it a try. Ben liked them and so did Bob and I. One of the local human service agencies that served people with severe disabilities agreed to work with us to figure out what Ben and his housemates needed. Bob and the executive director of this agency were old friends, and he knew her values were in line with ours, meaning that Ben and his housemates would be the leaders in determining what was needed and not needed. We all knew, also, that Ben needed some sort of work, but what would it be?

With the help of his housemates and the agency, Ben tried a number of different volunteer jobs, most of which were disasters. His autistic behaviors just kept getting in the way. When it finally occurred to us to ask Ben what he wanted to do we were literally stunned at his choice of career. But, once again, we felt we had to honor his wishes and do our best to see if being a woodworker was realistic. Could Ben develop the necessary skills? Could he be safe? Could we find someone to work with him who would help Ben, but not take over and do the work for him? Bob taught him how to use the necessary power tools and about six months later, Ben Lehr and Company opened for business. Ben has been building furniture now for over ten years. His skills have improved and his business has grown slowly but surely.

After a fire that destroyed his house in 2004, and his housemate of ten years moved on, Ben moved into a new home out of the city. Here he has a new larger shop for his business, a dream he had for a long time. Finding new housemates, however, was tortuous. There were several, but none stayed. Today, Ben lives alone (his choice), but has daily assistance from friends and family to help with meals, housecleaning, and life in general. The agency funds much of this through the Medicaid Waiver, but keeps this aspect of Ben's life to a minimum (also his wish).

Bob and I have retired and live about ten miles from Ben. We don't see him every day, but he does visit on occasion. He has his own life now, as do we. We all are still very close as a family. To assure that Ben's life, and that of our daughters, continues to be what it is, we have made very detailed wills, and established legal trusts to protect Ben and his home. We firmly believe that the decisions we made early in Ben's life were the right ones. We could never have predicted what happened along the way, but we do know that Ben's life is richer today because he has what he wants – a home, his work, his family and his friends.

Some of the names and places here are real. Some are not. Ben's words, as typed using facilitated communication, appear in capital letters. Our stories are real, they happened to us.

Chapter 1

TASTY

It was early evening. The supper dishes had been cleared from the table. Later we would stack them in the dishwasher. Right now it was homework time. The table was covered with textbooks, notepaper, and subject folders. Ben was sitting in his usual chair with his lap top computer ready in front of him.

"You have homework in Math and Health. Which do you want to do first?" Sherry, Ben's oldest sister, held out her hand to Ben. Using his left hand, he grasped her index finger and typed "H".

"Okay. Health it is." said Sherry.

"The assignment says to choose an object that best describes your personality and write a short essay telling how the object represents you." She waited and looked at Ben.

"What object do you think represents you?" Again, Sherry held out her hand. Ben sat for a few moments. Then a small grin appeared. He took Sherry's hand and began to type.

I AM FOOD.

WHAT KIND OF FOOD?

FOOD IN GENERAL.

FOOD IS TASTY.

He stopped typing.

"Is that all you want to write?" Sherry asked. Ben was still holding her finger. After each letter she had gently pulled his hand back away from the keyboard and waited patiently until he began to type again. Now she waited for his answer. Ben began again.

I AM TASTY.

I AM OPALESCENT.

I HAVE MANY FLAVORFUL SIDES.

MY BEST FLAVOR IS CAGED PHEASANT.

GO TO THE TURKEY FARM TO FIND OUT ABOUT CAGED PHEASANT.

He let go of Sherry's hand and sat back in his chair. His grin widened. We all smiled with Ben. We were delighted with his wit and creativity.

"Oh, my God." I thought. "What does this mean?" Rationally, I could make sense of some of it. It was Thanksgiving time. We had gone to the "turkey farm" the week before to get our turkey. We had gone through the exhibits of caged animals; baby ducks, turkeys, sheep, and calves. We had not seen any pheasants, at least not that I remembered. As I thought about that, I slowly realized that Ben's typed message had other deeper meanings, far more complex and complicated. We were at the brink of discovering a new, different Ben.

Emotionally, I was confused, scared, thrilled and curious. Ben had been labeled as having autism when he was four years old, and as he grew up, he certainly had lived up (or down, as the case may be) to this wretched diagnosis.

When he was sixteen, however, this all changed. Ben was introduced to a new and controversial form of assisted pointing or typing for people who could not speak. This new system, which was called facilitated communication, dramatically changed our lives and Ben's. It was a heady time, but we never could have predicted what eventually happened.

Chapter 2

Reflections on our life

As I stood in my kitchen that evening, I thought back about what a crazy life we have lived. I remember discretely watching Ben and Sherry complete his homework assignment. I thought about each one of them. Sherry, our oldest child, was born in 1968. She and Ben were very close despite being almost six years apart. She seemed to have an intuitive sense about what Ben needed or wanted, and how he felt. Even though he towered over her tiny five-foot frame, she could calm him with her gentle voice, sweet smile, and absolute love and acceptance of who he was. She was never afraid of him, but held high expectations that he would try to do his best, especially at controlling himself. She had been one of the first people to easily facilitate with Ben because she had full confidence in him.

Sherry had moved back home after graduating from college. She had a good job, but I knew it wouldn't be long before she moved on. She was already talking about graduate school.

How would I manage without her? I had missed her terribly when she left for college, a few years earlier, but I comforted myself by rationalizing that she was within a day's drive, and we talked on the phone frequently. I depended on her a lot to problem solve about Ben. I knew it was going to be very hard not just for me, but for Ben when she left.

Penny, our middle child, was just four months old when we adopted her in 1973. She and Ben were only twenty months apart in age. I wasn't sure how she felt about Ben. She tolerated him; at least it seemed that way to me. She talked to him and didn't ignore him, but she also seemed indifferent. Later she would explain to me,

"He was my little brother, what's the big deal?" I don't know. What did I expect?

Then I looked back at Ben and Sherry intently working on the computer. Her hand seemed to disappear as he gently curled the fingers of his left hand around her index finger, pointed his own index finger at the keyboard and began to push toward the letters. His eyes were fixed on the keyboard as were Sherry's, but I could see his index finger moving from side to side as he searched for the letter he wanted. After typing each letter he would pull his hand sharply back away from the keyboard before he began searching for the next letter. As he completed each word he would look up at the display screen. Sherry would hold his hand back until he was ready to type again. At the end of each sentence he would pull his hand away from Sherry's and put it in his lap. She often took this little break to shake her hand to regain some circulation, or rub her forearm where her muscles were stiffening. It looked so ordinary and yet what was happening was truly extraordinary.

Who would have believed that Ben could write, type, read, communicate this way? Certainly not us. It was 1986 when Ben wrote this assignment. Technically, this was his sophomore year in high school. Unlike the other autistic students in his high school, who were in separate special education classes, Ben attended regular classes with his non-disabled peers. By today's definitions, he would be placed in the "classical" end of the autism spectrum due to a lot of difficulties with speech, perception, motor skills, and control of his body. From the time Ben was diagnosed with autism until he began using facilitated communication twelve years later, Bob and I had tried to learn everything we could about autism, but most of the information was disturbing. It was expected that children like Ben would eventually be institutionalized because of their bizarre and often outrageous behaviors. This was totally unacceptable to us. We thought that we could make a good life for him. We knew he had limitations, but we wanted him to be happy and have as normal a childhood as we could provide. We wanted him to have opportunities to grow and learn. He wouldn't get that in an institution. We couldn't ignore his autism, but we weren't going to let it rule our family either.

I noticed Bob standing in the doorway, quietly watching his family. He had been trained as a behavioral psychologist so he found Ben's autistic behaviors both fascinating and frustrating. Facilitated communication, however, was really a conundrum for him. He believed it worked for some individuals, but was reluctant to believe Ben "had the smarts" to communicate this way. It only took a few validating messages to convince Bob that Ben was authoring his own words. Witnessing Ben describe himself as "opalescent" was one of these experiences.

"I'm not even sure what that word means, let alone know how to spell it." Bob commented later.

What is normal, anyway?

Until Ben started using facilitated communication, Bob and I had accepted the fact that Ben was probably also moderately mentally retarded. That's what the professional literature and most doctors said was associated with autism. Some professionals who knew Ben were convinced that he was severely retarded. They called it "severely intellectually impaired." I guess that was supposed to sound better than mentally retarded. Although there were instances when he surprised us with

Beautiful Ben

what he said or did, we learned not to consider him "normal" in the same way our other children were.

One spring afternoon Penny asked me about this. It was a disturbing question.

"Mom, do you ever wonder what Ben would be like if he was normal?" she asked. We were in her bedroom. She had gotten mad at Ben because he had ruined one of her favorite music tapes. I had run up the stairs when I heard her scream at him. She was standing in his bedroom with her fists clenched at her sides. Her face was contorted with anger and her eyes were brimming with tears. She spun around and ran down the hall to her bedroom, but she didn't slam the door shut. I hate conflict; I get anxious and sick feeling. I had witnessed too much screaming, yelling, violence growing up. I always tried to do something to avoid conflict. I leaned against her bedroom doorjamb, unsure of what to say or how to respond to her question. I wanted to make her feel better, and I guess I was trying to make myself feel better too. She was sitting on her bed, the remnants of the audiotape limply hanging from her fingers like cold spaghetti. She looked so glum. Her long dark hair curled around her face, hiding her eyes. I started to speak.

"Honey, I don't think Ben really meant to hurt you. It is just hard for him to..."

Her head snapped up and she glared at me with such intensity I was shocked, her beautiful grey eyes had turned dark. I held my breath.

"You're always making excuses for him," she almost whispered. She paused, and I took a slow deep breath, but my thoughts were interrupted when Penny repeated her question.

"Well, what would it be like if he were normal?" Her voice was sharp and edged with anger. It made me wonder, what would it be like? I comforted myself by thinking that at least I wasn't going to have to worry about him driving a car, or getting hurt while playing football, or maybe getting enticed into drugs. I was thankful he wouldn't be able to join the military. At least, I was safe from those "normal" worries that other parents had, or so I thought. I knew that these were not Penny's concerns. I had to say something to help her. I answered by saying something about how I thought Ben was normal "for Ben". It was the best I could think of. I had equivocated and she knew it. She glared at me.

"Ah, come on Mom, be real." The sarcasm dripped from every word. She shook her heard in resignation and looked away. I knew I had been dismissed. Quietly, I left her room. As I walked slowly back to Ben's room I thought about all the other problems that came as part of Ben's autism, but I knew I was learning how to handle these and I felt generally competent to be his mother. Moments like these, however, unnerved me.

I had never even heard of autism when we discovered that was what was making Ben's life so bizarre. We actually thought his problems were the result of a combination of other factors.

Chapter 3
What's happening to Ben?

Until Ben was almost one year old we didn't pay much attention to the fact that he was not achieving the traditional milestones that our other children had. We excused his slow development in a number of ways. We assumed that his prenatal care was probably poor. Since he was such a large baby it seemed natural that he would develop slowly. We also thought that boys generally developed at a slower rate than girls and since our first two children were girls we made allowances for Ben. We also thought that moving from foster care to our house, then a cross country move - well, so many major changes in one little guy's life must have had some sort of an impact. We went on with life. We were concerned, however, that his one eye was turned in. He wasn't crossed eyed, but his eye was definitely off.

"Maybe that's his problem. Poor Ben, he probably can't see very well and that's why he isn't doing some things." It was easy to make this excuse, especially since Ben's pediatrician suggested that he would outgrow this problem. He didn't give us any exercises to do with Ben, but when I finally persisted he did make a referral to a local ophthalmologist.

The ophthalmologist from hell...

Our one and only visit to the ophthalmologist was devastating. We waited in the reception area for a long time. I was thankful I had not brought Sherry and Penny along. They would have been restless. Ben was fussy too, but I didn't blame him. I was getting impatient when finally our name was called. We were shown into the examining room. A nurse and doctor were already there. Neither of them said anything, although I expected they would at least introduce themselves. The nurse pointed to a chair where I should sit. Ben was on my lap. She abruptly squirted some drops into his eyes. He winced. She shut off the lights in the examining room and, without saying a word, took Ben from my arms. She abruptly turned Ben upside down and thrust his head between her knees. Before I could protest the doctor shone a penlight into each of Ben's eyes. He took only seconds. Without looking directly at me, he said, "This child is brain damaged. There is nothing I can do for him." He walked out of the room. The nurse handed Ben back to me, flipped on the lights as she also left the room. I was stunned. I went absolutely numb.

I don't remember leaving the office. I don't even remember driving home. All I can remember is the shock and the pain. I had specifically selected this man because he was highly regarded, was African American, and was willing to treat young children. I thought he would be sensitive and caring, thoughtful and gentle. He was none of these. He was rude, arrogant, and mean. I was totally devastated. This man, this professional, was so inhumane to Ben and me. I felt violated and betrayed. I sobbed as I told Bob what had happened.

"What do we do now?" was all I could say.

"Mommy, why are you crying?" The look on Sherry's face was bewildered. I don't think she had ever seen me cry before.

"I don't know, honey. I honestly don't know." was all I could muster. Later, when I had calmed down, I thought back to when we had adopted Ben. It was not planned at all.

Chapter 4

Adopting Ben

When Penny was about one year old, Bob accepted a year-long sabbatical leave from his teaching position, and we moved to Utah where he would work with a respected behavioral psychologist who was researching a new aspect of learning behavior. We were excited about this new adventure. We had no intentions, at that time, of adopting any more children, but we did contact the local adoption agency to see what their requirements and procedures were. We had friends in New York who were hoping they might be able to arrange for interstate adoptions and we told them we would see what we could learn on their behalf.

We met with an adoption caseworker after explaining what we were trying to accomplish, and reiterating that were not personally interested in adopting another child. Right now, having two small children was challenging enough. We simply wanted to help families back in New York who were eager to do so. We told her about our family and what our friends were hoping for. She asked questions and said she would make some inquiries. She gave us some pamphlets and told us she would be in touch. It was a nice visit and we left not really expecting much more. A few days later, however, she did call back, but it wasn't what I had expected to hear.

Adopt another kid? Now?

"Mrs. Lehr, we have a little baby boy, five months old, who has been placed with us for adoption. He is biracial. We need to find him a home, and I immediately thought of you and your family. Would you be interested in discussing placement with me?"

I was speechless. We had made it quite clear that we were not interested in adoption, but I felt compelled to listen - who was this little guy? Being biracial I could figure out why he had been placed for adoption. I was curious, however, to know more about him. I think already, deep in my heart, I knew we would take him. I scheduled an appointment to learn more. We met with the caseworker again, but this time the agenda was different. We were going to be moving back to New York within a month. Should we, could we, adopt another child? We had so many questions.

The next three weeks were a whirlwind of activity. My suspicions about why he had been placed for adoption were confirmed when we were told that he had been surrendered at birth because of his racial heritage, and because his unmarried parents were teenagers. The agency knew it would next to impossible to find any adoptive parents who wanted a "baby like him." We hadn't planned on this, but we also felt we couldn't say "no". Bob remembers thinking that the description of this little boy sounded so similar to Penny.

"Here was this poor kid, stuck in Utah-land as a biracial kid. What else could we do?" Even though we had not seen him or held him, we agreed to adopt him. At the time, of course, we didn't know that Ben had any handicaps or disabilities.

Before we adopted Penny, we had talked about adopting handicapped children. I dismissed the idea almost immediately. That was not where my heart was, nor did I think I could do it - mother a handicapped child.

"I just don't think I could handle it. I remember watching my mother struggle with Eddie. Remember him, my retarded cousin? I wouldn't be able to do the right thing. I am sure of that." Eddie had lived in a special residential school near us, but far from his parents. He came to visit us often and I remember the problems he presented to my mother. I loved him. He had a winsome way that made me feel special, but he could be so annoying too. He drooled a lot and had such a goofy laugh. Sometimes he had temper tantrums that were almost scary. He was bigger than me and heavy. When we went to the pool I was embarrassed by how fat he was and how awkward. He was two years older, but when I turned 14 he gave me a pretty bracelet with two little hearts on it. It was such a sweet gesture of love. I knew he had selected it himself, and I was touched by his thoughtfulness. Even though I felt sorry for him, it certainly didn't mean I wanted a kid like him. Of course, I didn't even consider that we might be adopting a child like my cousin. I was so naïve.

Welcome to our family, Ben.

On May 8, 1974, less than three weeks later we drove north to the place where the adoption agency had directed us. It was a big old house in a small town far away from where we had met the adoption caseworker. When we entered the front door, we had no idea what would happen. Sherry was holding my hand and clutching a small stuffed squirrel and Bob was carrying Penny. We all were wide-eyed and nervous. The waiting room reminded me an old-fashioned parlor. There were overstuffed chairs, a bit threadbare, a sofa, lamps and magazines on end tables, and an old oriental rug on the floor. It felt homey. I looked around at the

Beautiful Ben

other people, wondering if they were there for the same reason. My thoughts were interrupted by the receptionist who greeted us.

"Good Morning. May I help you?"

"Yes. Thank you. We are the Lehrs." As soon as she heard our name she stood and turned away from the waiting room. She quietly explained that as soon as we were ready she would show us into a private room where we would find the child. She gestured toward a door not far from her desk. Continuing in her soft voice, she explained that we would be in the room alone with him.

"Take as much time as you need to reach your decision. Feel free to pick him up if you like. If you decide you want to keep him, dress him in the clothes you have brought. You did bring some clothes, didn't you?" She looked kind, but nervous. I held up a small bag that contained the outfit. She nodded and smiled. Then she continued.

"If you want to keep him, change his clothes and then leave by the door at the end of the room. Later your case worker will contact you about the next steps." We waited. She swallowed quietly, paused, and then went on.

"If you decide not to take him, return to the reception area. I'll be right here. Then you are free to leave. Are you ready? Do you understand the directions?" We nodded silently. She showed us into a small dimly lit room and asked us to sit on the bench.

There was an old cradle, just inches away from our knees. Our eyes became adjusted to the dim light and we saw a huge baby sleeping on his back in the cradle. He wore only a disposable diaper. It was the weirdest feeling, to look at him like we were deciding on buying a new car or something. I could hear the baby breathing. Sherry and Penny were very quiet, looking at him. I don't know what they were thinking, but I had this silly thought about how they would think this is where babies came from.

"Some did." I thought, But how was I going to explain this to them?

I pushed these thoughts from my mind and squeezed Bob's hand. I don't know what any of us expected. I was really shocked when I first looked at him closely. He looked so Black. He had big lips. He was totally bald and his huge body nearly filled the small cradle. Penny never looked like that. She was much smaller and delicate looking. His skin was beautiful, soft and brown. My mind was racing.

"I want you for my son. I know that. I don't know who you are yet, but you are mine." I knew Bob agreed. We exchanged looks and smiled; we knew what we were going to do. We sat there for a few minutes, I am not sure how many, and then we quietly dressed him, although the outfit was a bit small. He was much bigger than I had expected for such a young baby; barely five months old. I picked him up and nestled him in my arms. He stirred, but didn't fully awake. Sherry gently took hold of his toes and smiled up at us. Bob picked up Penny and I carried this new son with Sherry tagging along, still clutching her little squirrel. Quietly, we left by the back door.

"Wow. He's heavy." I whispered.

We gently laid this new baby boy in a port-a-crib in the back of our van. He opened his eyes, but he was totally silent. He just stared and lay in the crib. His eyes were like huge, deep brown pools. Both Penny and Sherry had brought toys and they put these in the port-a-crib. They hung over the sides of the crib and talked, telling their new brother about the toys, our house, their bedroom and what it would be like to live with us. We drove away and went to a local park. Sherry and Penny played on the playground equipment and Bob and I wondered if we had any idea what we were doing. Of course we didn't, but we thought we were doing the right thing.

We named our new son Ben. It was a strong name. Because we had decided that we wanted to call him Ben we never even considered using the more formal title of "Benjamin". Just like Sherry and Penny, we didn't give him a middle name. We figured that if any of our children wanted to choose a new name later in life, there would be a natural space to add it. I will not lie and say that we loved this new addition instantly. It took some time, but not much.

I would whisper in his ear, "I love your soft brown skin – your beautiful brown skin. I love you, my beautiful Ben." I still tell him that. Although he hardly had any hair, he sprouted a little topknot of curly golden brown hair, kind of like a Mohawk cut. His soft tummy was like chocolate pudding and I loved to tickle and kiss him gently on his tummy. He was a beautiful child, so gentle and quiet, easy even, maybe too easy. After Penny, however, this was a bit of a relief. He seemed happy and that is what mattered most to me.

Ben had lived in foster care since birth. The adoption case worker described him as a healthy baby, weighing in at 9 pounds 11 ounces at birth with "normal APGAR scores". His parents were young and unmarried, one was white and Mormon, one was black. Because of the speed of the placement, however, his birth and subsequent medical records were not complete. The agency promised to forward them as soon as they could. We believed them. We trusted them. We didn't understand that he had been surrendered to a different agency initially and that his records were located elsewhere. No one told us this. We thought the agency

Beautiful Ben

representatives were honest with us when they told us his birth was ordinary and that he was a normal, healthy baby boy. It was much later before we learned that their initial "normal" determination was incorrect.

Within a few weeks of bringing Ben home we were headed back to New York State, now with three children. The trip home was quite an adventure. We headed north into Canada with letters and documentation of Ben's adoption, just in case we were questioned at the border. We weren't. Having two kids in diapers was daunting, but within a day of leaving Utah, Ben developed diarrhea. He wasn't particularly fussy, and I felt I spent almost every minute changing diapers. Thank God for disposables.

We had fun, however, traversing the Canadian Rockies, seeing glaciers for the first time, and all kinds of fascinating birds. Sherry and Penny acclimated quickly to their new brother, describing what they saw.

"Look at that." Sherry would point to a big tree or a puffy cloud. Penny would quickly repeat "Dook. Dook, Ben." And she too pointed off into space. Bob and I smiled. This was going to be fun. It took us a couple of weeks, because we wanted to sight see as we went. We arrived home in time for Bob to prepare for the fall semester while I unpacked the house and prepared for Sherry to enter second grade. We had no idea what was coming.

Now, however, less than a year later, we were confronted with a potential diagnosis of brain damage and little else. Could this be true? Maybe the ophthalmologist was wrong. What did we know about Ben's birth and prenatal care? Maybe there would be something in those records that would help Ben, help us to know what to do. Bob and I talked into the wee hours of the morning trying to decide what we should do.

Time for Action – but what should we do?

We were forced to look at Ben from a different perspective now. What we saw both shocked and saddened us. At eight months Ben could sit alone, but only if we put him in that position. Otherwise he would remain on his back, content to play with his toes or flip his fingers in front of his eyes. By one year, Ben was not really crawling; nor was he making consistent attempts to pull himself to a standing position. If supported, he would take a step or two, but he rarely initiated any of this. Bob recognized that Ben was not achieving some significant developmental milestones.

We had to do something. I called our attorney in Utah, the one who had finalized Ben's adoption. I explained what was happening and begged him to help us get whatever information was in the adoption agency records. He was sympathetic, but said it would take time. He would get back to me once he knew something. I just couldn't wait. I didn't know how long it would take. I also felt that time was becoming very important. I felt helpless.

One way I channel my fear and anger in situations like this is to write letters, carefully worded, thoughtful letters; letters with a point that demands action or answers. This one was addressed to the adoption agency.

"We took Ben to the doctor's and found that they have not received any medical records for Ben. It is absolutely essential that we receive the medical records on Ben. We have reason to believe that Ben's development is retarded and we cannot properly evaluate his progress unless we know as much as possible about his birth and early development." (January, 1975.)

Further on, we described his development by saying, "...his gross motor development is the area that has concerned us the most...until recently, he did not make eye contact with us", but we had attributed this to his turned in eye.

"The ophthalmologist felt there was no physical damage to the eye...if there was a visual difficulty it was because of brain damage. This diagnosis, in addition to our pediatrician's concerns and our general apprehensions had all led to the realization that Ben's development is retarded." And then we waited for the attorney in Utah to respond, or for the agency to do something. We wanted to know what we should do to help Ben.

In the meantime our pediatrician referred us to a local early childhood evaluation center for a comprehensive assessment. Why hadn't he said anything sooner? He told us he was waiting for us to ask him.

"Good grief! What if we had never asked? How long would you have waited?" There was no answer. We scheduled an appointment. We had no expectations other than hoping they could give us some ideas of what we should do to help Ben gain new skills like crawling and walking. We weren't looking for a specific diagnosis, just some ideas and suggestions of what we should do. We hadn't considered that there was anything really "wrong" with Ben. We just wanted guidance about how to help him develop.

A few weeks later, a team of specialists including a psychologist, speech therapist, physical therapist and medical doctor, met with us and examined Ben. It took the better part of a day. Little was said after the session was over. We all were exhausted and assumed that we would hear something once they had analyzed their findings. We also assumed they would send us some sort of a report or

Beautiful Ben

schedule another appointment to discuss their findings and maybe some strategies. We never received anything written or verbal. Time passed. How long? I don't remember, but it seemed an eternity. Finally, in desperation we demanded to know what they had found. They informed us that their report had been forwarded to Ben's pediatrician.

"What? When?"

"Not very long after the evaluation."

"Why wasn't the report, or at least a copy, sent to us?" I asked. I was politely, but firmly informed that because Bob and I were "just parents", not professionals, that this was their procedure. They were afraid that we might misinterpret the technical data and test scores. They expected our pediatrician to explain these to us. It was a professional courtesy. Our pediatrician had made the referral. It was his responsibility to interpret the report and decide what to share with us.

"Bob has a Ph.D. in Psychology!" I almost shouted it into the phone.

"I'm sorry, Mrs. Lehr. You need to discuss this with Ben's pediatrician. He will be able to explain what the results mean." Her voice seemed so patronizing. I was furious.

"Why can't you all do that?" It was a question that was left unanswered.

"Please, Mrs. Lehr, call your pediatrician." I did, but I didn't really expect anything anymore. We hadn't heard from our attorney; the adoption agency was silent. Who was going to tell us what was going on? Who would tell us the truth? Who would tell us how to help Ben?

Our pediatrician met with us, but what he had to say told us nothing. The general recommendation of the assessment team was that we should continue our "active stimulation training" (whatever that was), get a full medical screening, and have a physical therapy evaluation. I wasn't quite sure what they meant by stimulation training. We were actively playing with Ben, trying to teach him what we thought he should know. As part of a class project, three of Bob's psychology students were coming to our house 3-4 times a week to help Ben learn how to hold a spoon and feed himself.

The students started by covering Ben's high chair tray with whipped cream into which they dropped plastic toys and spoons. They made a game of trying to find these and then showed Ben how to lick the whipped cream from his fingers. They modeled for him and became quite animated when they found something. In the beginning they had to hold his hand and guide him in searching. He wasn't too keen on getting his hands into the whipped cream, but he did like the taste of it. That was a start. Later they gave him a small spoon and hand-over-hand helped him scoop some whipped cream from the tray into his mouth. Was this "active stimulation therapy"? I had no idea.

A few days later we received a written report from the assessment team, forwarded by our pediatrician. In the report the team noted that "parents indicated ...that they do not want him in a program". During the course of the assessment of Ben they had suggested that he might benefit from an intensive early intervention special education program. We explained that we weren't ready for that. We were still trying to figure out what we could do. The report acknowledged this and then went on to say, ..."Ben's difficulties are probably secondary to the fetal distress and birth difficulties." We were confused. What "fetal distress"? What had happened during his birth process? We had been told that everything was normal. The report suggested that Bob and I should consider professional counseling to help us deal with Ben's problems. They noted that they thought that maybe we were expecting too much. Were we? We didn't think so. If fact, we thought we should expect Ben to progress and grow.

I remembered one of the team members advising us to "Go home and enjoy your little baby boy. Just accept him as he is."

"What does that mean?" I wondered. It was all so overwhelming. We needed time to think, to regroup, and to decide what to do. Our pediatrician was no help. He just shrugged his shoulders and complimented us on what dedicated parents we were. Even worse, I felt that we were being dismissed or written off as too demanding. I tried to think clearly about what had happened. The adoption agency had either withheld information about Ben's birth or they had openly lied to us (later we learned they didn't have any records). The ophthalmologist had diagnosed brain damage. I wondered if he was qualified to do this. The staff at the evaluation center had not made significant recommendations about what we could do to help Ben, just Freudian suggestions that we were the ones who really needed help. Maybe we did, but how would that help Ben? I felt like they made us out to be "the bad guys" because we were not ready to plunge Ben into a "program." It wasn't that we objected to the idea of therapies and interventions, it was more that we wanted to know what they were and how we could do them with Ben in our home, not in some "center". That was all we really wanted, but later I began to realize that they were the "professionals" and we were "just parents". In their eyes, we were not professionally trained or qualified to engage Ben in therapeutic activities. And we weren't ready to turn Ben over to them either.

What do we do now?

We were relieved when the evaluation center contacted us and offered to send someone to our house once a week for a half hour to give us ideas on ways to play with Ben, engage him physically and verbally.

"Okay. Let's start with this. At least it should give us some ideas of what to do on a daily basis." We wanted some hope.

The physical therapist was supposed to show me strategies for helping Ben develop his motor skills so he could stand and walk, grasp toys and utensils, utter sounds. It didn't take me long to realize that her protocol of activities were totally unrelated to where Ben was developmentally. I finally ended up showing her the strategies I was using. She would watch me, write in her notebook, and then leave.

On more than one occasion she commented, "Oh, that's a good idea. I hadn't thought of that."

"Argh!!!!!!" I began to feel that we were wasting our time and worse, Ben was not really progressing, although he was content. I kept hoping that these sessions would be productive, but ultimately I concluded they were worthless and a waste of time. It was definitely time to find out what had happened during Ben's birth.

We contacted our attorney in Utah again, but he had had not found anything. I wondered how hard he had tried. In total frustration and desperation, we called the surrendering adoption agency and demanded that his birth and medical records be sent immediately. Although I wasn't able to speak to our original caseworker, someone else listened to my story. This time I emphasized that Ben appeared to be delayed and we needed any information that could help us decide what to do. I told her our attorney would be contacting them also seeking this information. I actually wasn't sure about this, but I thought the implied threat couldn't hurt.

The caseworker told us she would investigate and call us back. We tried to be patient, but it was so hard. We wanted information, some answers, some sort of explanation, something we could do. We were scared too. What had happened to Ben at birth?

Within a few days the director of the agency, not the caseworker, called. She informed us that our caseworker had "left that agency and the state." She explained. "Unfortunately, when there is a change in staff, things get bogged down. I will make an effort to contact the doctors directly, as soon as I can learn who he or they are. This may take a little time, but I hope that you can be patient." What choice did we have?

Not long after, she called again to say "We received the medical information on Ben...Unfortunately, the information is not good. Ben had a difficult delivery, was born breach, and was finally delivered with the aid of a vacuum. His apgar rating was two and five, which is another indication of fetal distress during delivery." She explained that Ben was not breathing at birth and needed resuscitation in order to breathe. We were stunned.

"Why didn't they tell us this in the beginning? I told them we didn't want a handicapped kid! How the hell do you deliver a baby weighing almost ten pounds by a vacuum; a baby in a breach position? I immediately thought of Ben's birth mother. She must have been terrified. My heart went out to her, but now I had to focus on Ben and what to do.

The director called again, a few days later. She was very gracious and apologetic about what had happened to Ben. She was deeply sorry for the trauma he and everyone involved had endured, but she felt her agency had acted in good faith when they placed Ben with us.

"We will stand behind the placement, and if you desire, we will fly a worker to New York to pick him up."

What? What was happening? They were taking him back? Could they do this? I was numb. My thoughts were all over the place. I remember thinking, at the time, that she was describing Ben as if he were a sweater I had bought that had a flaw, a snag, a tear. I could return it for credit, or exchange it.

"This is our son you are talking about.." My voice was low and flat. I was in shock.

"We're not sending him back! We want information. We want to know what you know." I hung up the phone.

Later, she would write, "It is not our impression that this is what you want, but in all fairness to your family, we want to give you a way out. We will abide by the decision that you make."

A way out??? What did that mean? What was she not telling us? Of course we were going to keep Ben! He was our son, and he was going to stay!! No matter what! We had made that decision the moment we said "Yes, we will adopt him." We were not going to send him back, ever! But, what was ahead? We went back to the evaluation center. Now that we all knew more about Ben's birth, could they help us?

Our first hint of autism

The consultant psychologist from the evaluation center eventually saw Ben on three different occasions. In her third report, when Ben was just turning three, she noted, "one would have to say that there are many autistic characteristics present." Her summary stated, "These include a lack of appropriate responsiveness to the human figure, avoidance of eye contact, stereotyped body contact and a tendency to relate to the human figure in terms of parts of the body. Ben has also had considerable language delay and deviation. His expressive language has been slow in development and much of his present language is echolalia. Ben does not respond appropriately to language without additional tactical stimulation..."

Later she would add, "Ben is functionally retarded and is going to need a lot of special educational attention." She praised us for our efforts with Ben, noting that these had been helpful although his progress seemed minimal. She again noted that she wanted to see Ben placed in a preschool special education program so that the "parent stimulation and involvement" would be supplemented.

"It is difficult to be a teacher as well as a parent and while Ben's parents have done an excellent job they really should have some external support through the public school system at this point," she recommended.

"A special school? It seemed so punitive. He hasn't done anything wrong. He is just a little boy." I cried at the notion of Ben being sent away like my cousin Eddie, or being isolated in the back wards of some "special school" or institution.

I vowed that, "No one is going to send him to one of those awful back wards in some gross institution."

I'd seen them. I had been inside their walls. As a young child I had lived next door to Deveraux, (an institution for people who were blind and deaf – like Helen Keller, and who were thought to be mentally retarded). I'd even been to Willowbrook, a huge institution that later would be exposed as a hellhole, dirty, demeaning, and disgusting. Thanks to Geraldo Rivera, an investigate news reporter, and Bernard Carabello, a former inmate, society learned what egregious violations of human dignity occurred in the name of "treatment". My son was not going there or any other place like that.

I wouldn't let this happen! I was screaming, but who was listening? Bob was. He had been there, too. He knew the inhumanity and indignities perpetrated in the name of psychological treatment or punishment. He knew there were other options, ones that I didn't know much about. He was also more rational than I was. He knew that she was not recommending that we send Ben away. She was suggesting something quite different, but I didn't understand that then. Because of Bob's involvement with ARC and other programs and agencies, and his professional background in psychology, he knew of a wider range of options. He calmed me down. He held me as I sobbed.

"There has to be something else we can do." I cried. But what? Where?

Chapter 5

The Campus Laboratory School – a place for Ben?

There was. Bob told me about it. The Campus Laboratory School at SUNY Cortland, where Sherry and Penny were receiving an excellent education also had a classroom for "handicapped" children ages three and four.

"I haven't visited this particular classroom, but I do hear good things about it. Besides, it is located in a school where many people can witness what is going on. Our Psych students are assigned there. It might be good. All we can do is look and see. Let's at least look. Okay?"

We visited the room, met the teacher and the classroom aide. We were impressed. I was encouraged at how sweet and sensitive Miss Blanchard was. She was very organized and it soon became apparent that every lesson, every detail of the classroom day, was thoughtfully planned to build on the existing competencies of each child as well as lay the foundation for developing new skills. Her lessons were fun. The kids were enthusiastic, but not wild. Order was built into the structure of the lessons while even "free time" was organized around play centers that engaged the kids in sensory motor play. At times the room was noisy, but not chaotic, while at other times it was quiet and peaceful. Could I see Ben fitting in here? I wasn't sure.

Miss Blanchard explained the curriculum and her approach to teaching. She was young, but she was clear about what she wanted from her children. She had high expectations and higher standards for herself and her staff. As we watched the children engage in structured activities and then in free play, we saw opportunities where Ben could learn and grow. We were also encouraged to find out that Sherry and Penny were welcome to pop into the room anytime they wanted to visit their brother.

"Tell them to bring their friends, just not too many at one time." Miss Blanchard explained that having other children there to play with her students was good for everyone. She also told us that there were undergraduate students from different disciplines who visited to observe or participate with the children. Sometimes they led an activity.

"Everyone learns from each other. It is really a win-win situation. It is just good for everyone."

We were invited too, and since Bob was a faculty member in the Psychology Department on the same campus, Miss Blanchard encouraged him to bring his students.

"If and when appropriate, there is an observation room behind that one-way mirror. Your students might benefit from seeing how our children develop. Of course, you are welcome to observe anytime too." She smiled warmly at both of us. I was beginning to relax. Maybe this was the right decision. Ben would receive speech therapy, physical therapy, and self help skill training. He would be with other kids too. That might help his social development. It seemed promising and, to be honest, we were ready to latch onto anything that might help Ben.

But, we needed help too, Bob and I. We had joined the local ARC – then it was called the Association for Retarded Children. There we found other parents who were struggling with their "retarded" children who didn't seem to fit into the normal world as we knew it then. We found it comforting to talk with them and share our stories. We learned through them that, collectively, we could have power to change things that we thought were unjust or wrong. Bob was invited to become a board member of the Cortland ARC and willingly agreed. As he has throughout our life together, he brought balance and rationality to the emotional upheavals that we all faced. Because our keenest interest was in education, Bob quickly ascended to the chairmanship of the education committee at the state ARC level. He was respected for his well thought out positions, and valued for his commitment to improving the lives of all our children. He understood that some parents would resist the notion that their children were capable of more than segregated classrooms, sheltered workshops, and institutions or group homes. He understood that these ideas were scary and involved risks they were not prepared to accept. He tried to ask them to recognize that the path they were choosing, the segregated route, was also fraught with risks and dangers. They listened to him respectively. Some agreed, while some did not. Most parents in ARC were not able to move this far yet. They fully believed that their children would be protected and safe in these sheltered, segregated settings. Bob acknowledged their feelings and fears. He understood them. In turn, these parents respected Bob because he was a parent, just like them, and because they had heard our story. They knew Ben was not easy. He had a lot of behaviors that challenged us at every turn, but we were not about to give up on him or our belief that he could lead a good life among his non-disabled peers. I think Bob had a profound and lasting impact on the policies and actions of these organizations.

Our immediate concern, however, was getting Ben enrolled in this laboratory special program. He met the age criterion, but also had to be toilet trained. Here was a real challenge for all of us. Unlike his older sisters he didn't seem the slightest bit uncomfortable with a messy diaper. In fact, he showed no interest in learning to use the toilet. Bob, our resident experimental psychologist by training, set about reading the literature to find a way of toilet training Ben. It didn't take him long to design a systematic plan. In our family, however, it seems we never do anything really simply. That summer before Ben was to begin in the "handicapped preschool" program, we went on an extended camping trip, sleeping in tents, exploring the United States. It was on this trip that Ben learned how to use the potty.

We bought a little potty chair that looked like a cowboy's saddle and made sure it was always visible in our van or at our campsite. We would sit Ben on the "saddle" routinely and entertain him with blowing bubbles or pouring water from a glass bottle into a dishpan. He loved these interludes and it didn't take long for "something" to happen in the potty. Bob also took Ben with him whenever he went to the bathroom, even if it was simply a "one holer" outhouse. He wanted Ben to see how guys go to the bathroom. When Ben did go in the potty, we all made a big deal about it. We would applaud, sing songs, give him hugs and kisses. He seemed to enjoy this ruckus.

By the time school started in September of 1978, Ben was pretty successful with toileting, especially if he was taken routinely to the bathroom. Mrs. Green, the classroom aide in his new classroom commented later that he especially liked to wash his hands under the running water, but seemed to fear using a bar of soap. This was a curious observation, which we thought related to our using water to entertain him when we were camping. The fear of soap didn't make much sense to us. Later we thought about how we usually had a wet washcloth for his hands that we carried in a plastic bag.

Although he was toilet trained, when Ben began in this class he could not do some of the other simple self-help skills that most children his age found easy. He did not know colors; he seemed unable to recognize either of us when in a crowd, and he rarely attempted to interact with other children. In fact he never even looked at them. He seemed to stay in his own world. He didn't speak much except to repeat the last word someone had said. On occasion he would utter sounds, really just silly noises. He didn't communicate with us at all; at least we didn't recognize his efforts at communication. He could walk now, but his gait was awkward and he held his hands out in front of him, never swinging them in cadence with his gait. He seemed so aloof and isolated from us all so that we wondered if he knew we were there.

Often, Ben liked to rock back and forth and flip his fingers in front of his eyes. He would put one foot in front of the other and rock gently, sometimes violently. Occasionally, he still does this although now it usually it is an indicator of anxiety or confusion. As a small child, however, it appeared to be his way of entertaining himself. It felt good and the finger flipping was undoubtedly stimulating visually. This was Ben's way of "playing," or entertaining himself.

"What is going on in his mind? What is he thinking? What does he need? What does he want?" We didn't have any answers. We hoped this experience in preschool would help us begin to find some. Although, earlier, we had rejected the idea of a "program" we now looked forward to this as a way of discovering Ben and how to help him.

Individually and together, we visited Ben's class as often as we could. We went on field trips with the class. We listened, watched, learned from Miss Blanchard and Mrs. Green, the aide. We saw things that we liked and we learned about strategies for helping Ben to progress in his daily life. We witnessed other things, however, that were disquieting. Ben just was not like any of the other children. Donny, a small boy with Down Syndrome, seemed to be Ben's constant companion. The other children seemed to be progressing academically and socially, while Ben and Donny seemed stuck at some lower level of development. Eventually we learned each child had his or her own unique special education needs which demanded intensive attention and intervention. Then there was Ben. He was content to go off on his own away from the group. He liked to stare out the window or stand in the middle of a table and flap his fingers. Miss Blanchard quickly learned, too, that if the classroom door was left open Ben would quietly walk out and head down the hall. For the most part, however, Ben didn't interfere with anyone; he just did his own thing. It was easy to ignore him, lose him, in the chaos of the daily routines.

Miss Blanchard and Mrs. Green worked hard to plan and program for each of their ten pupils. Ben was no exception, but something didn't feel right to us. We would talk about this for hours, but we just couldn't put our finger on what was bothering us. We waited, hoping to grasp some sort of meaning or insight.

Miss Blanchard left at the end of the year. She was getting married and moving away. She was Ben's first teacher and we were devastated when she left. A new teacher was hired and, although her style was a bit different, we quickly recognized that Ms. Patrick was a solid, competent and skilled preschool teacher. She structured her lessons so that Ben had to participate, and she supported any effort he made. Halfway through this second year of preschool, when Ben was five, she confessed,

"Ben is just a conundrum to me. On the one hand, I see him as educable. You know, he could learn academic things like colors and shapes, maybe even some pre-reading skills. But just when I have convinced myself of this, I see him falter. I

Beautiful Ben

think to myself, 'No, he is only trainable." I mean, I think I can train him to do simple daily living skill things like wash his hands, brush his teeth, zip his fly. At these moments, I am not sure he can learn more." She looked at us as if we had the answers. We didn't, but we understood what she was trying to say.

That night Bob and I talked for hours, trying to put into words what we had been witnessing, experiencing, feeling over the past year and a half. We talked about Ben's future; where would he be in ten, twenty, thirty years? We talked about how scared we were to see him become isolated within his own cohort – his classroom. We recognized that he was becoming more retarded – what ever that meant. Maybe it meant that he just wasn't making any progress. He seemed content. Happy? We weren't sure, but we could see that was not able to do what other children his age could do. We saw him being left to the mercy of the teachers. His teachers, so far, had cared about him. What would happen if he had a teacher who didn't?

Perhaps, most provocative, was our slowly developing recognition that Ben would never survive if left in an isolated, special education world. Although he was only in preschool, we began asking each other the truly hard questions about his future. What will happen after this? From his experiences with other parents in the ARC, Bob knew that Ben would eventually be enrolled in an elementary special ed class, probably at BOCES (Board of Cooperative Educational Services) a local segregated campus where children were grouped according to their disability. Where would they put him? He couldn't go into the room for physically handicapped students. He didn't have Down Syndrome. What about the "MR" room, for mentally retarded kids? But even these were separated into mild, moderate and severe/profound groups. Did Ben really fit into any of these? There was also a room for emotionally disturbed children, but it never occurred to us that Ben might be assigned there. We had never perceived him as disturbed, just different. No matter which class he would end up in we kept wondering, " What will he learn there?" Bob knew from having some of his students do class projects or internships at this center, that job training was introduced when the student was about ten or eleven.

"To do what?" I asked innocently. "What kind of jobs do they get?"

"Work in a sheltered workshop. You know, like at the ARC workshop, or the one at BOCES. They do assembly line work or piece-work like putting holiday ornaments in boxes. You know. Something like that. After they finish school at BOCES, usually the ARC or some other sheltered workshop hires them and then they can get paid. Of course, the money is minimal, just pocket change really, because they aren't really doing the load of a regular worker, and there is something about not jeopardizing their social security checks. I don't know very much about that."

Bob continued as I listened with a deepening sense of doom. "I've visited the ARC workshop a few times. I was given the grand tour when I first went on the ARC Board of Directors. It wasn't so bad." He paused as if thinking about his visit.

"Really…it was awful. I hate to think of Ben going there. It is totally a dead end." We were sitting in our living room drinking wine. The sun was slowly setting, usually a special time for us, but today the gloom that settled into the room reflected how we were feeling. Even when we switched on the lights, we felt cold – and sad.

We didn't talk more about this for several days, but we both could not push these images from our minds. As an ARC Board member, Bob was also involved in their efforts to purchase a house, just around the corner from ours. The ARC had applied to the state to open a group home for adult retarded men. I was asked to make curtains for the bedrooms, and help buy sheets and towels.

"Oh yes, and can you see if you can collect some canned goods from some of your neighbors, just to get us started. Watch for rakes and things at garage sales too. We are really starting from scratch," said Martha, the mother of one of the young men who was slated to move into this new home. She was excited at the prospect for her son. She and her husband were getting older and it was becoming harder for them to manage, especially since Peter needed a lot of help with simple skills like bathing and dressing. She literally threw herself into getting the house ready. She and I had been friends so I didn't hesitate when she asked me to help. Her enthusiasm was catching too, but now I began to think of this house as the place where Ben might eventually live. This thought sobered me. Although I was happy for Martha and Peter, I was sick at the prospect of Ben living in a place like that. I knew how some of the neighbors had protested the idea.

"We don't want those retards near our kids." One man had shouted angrily at a public forum. Another woman had noted, "This is a neighborhood, not a hospital zone. Why can't they live somewhere else?"

"Yea. Why can't they?" Others nodded in agreement.

This wasn't what we wanted for Ben either. Weeks later, Bob and I were once again having our evening "wine time" as we now called it. Our conversations over the past several nights had returned to discussions of Ben, his schooling, his future.

"If he goes to BOCES, people will expect that he should eventually live in a group home with a lot of other retarded people. Don't get me wrong. There are people and families who choose this lifestyle, who want it for its security, but not me! I don't want that for Ben. How will he feel about himself? How will Sherry and Penny feel if we choose this? How will we feel? " I was pacing all around the living room, my wine sloshing over the edges of my glass as Bob and I bombarded each other with these questions.

"We just have to believe that Ben can do more. We have to believe his future is not going to be that dismal. We have to try!" I finished my glass of wine in one gulp.

"Sue, slow down." Bob was gesturing to me, slowly drawing his hands down over his chest, the way we often did for Ben when he was agitated.

"Come on. Take a breath. We need to talk this through." How I loved this man! He could bring rationality to my craziness, calmness to my hysteria. He poured me another glass of wine and we began to talk calmly, rationally, thoughtfully.

"Okay. We know we don't want Ben to be segregated into a "special education" world." Bob's voice was deep and serious.

"We want him to be among his peers, but not his handicapped peers. That means...," he paused as he collected his thoughts, "... we want him to be with kids his own age in the same classroom and activities. Right?"

"Yes, that's it." I thought about what we had been reading about "inclusion" (educating children like Ben in the regular education classroom) and the implications of the new law, P.L. 94-142, which had just been passed by Congress in 1975. It included a clause about educating children with disabilities, kids like Ben, in the "least restrictive environment" – that was the regular education classroom. I thought about my cousin, and all the marginalized kids I had taught. I thought about the ARC parents and children. I thought about Ben. Yes! I just wanted Ben to have an equal chance. I was willing to fight for that! Bob understood, and he agreed. We didn't need to talk about this anymore. We knew it was right, just like it had been right to adopt Penny and Ben. Now we just had to figure out how to do it. That, we soon learned, was not going to be easy.

Chapter 6

Discovering the autism lurking within Ben

Our first indication of what would later be called autism occurred when Ben was still an infant, no more than 6-7 months old, but we didn't recognize it. We had been living in Utah for about a year and were preparing to move back to New York State. One weekend we had a rummage sale. Friends, who had a baby boy about the same age as Ben, came to help us. They sat Jason next to Ben, each in their own infant seats. We were busy trying to sell our old furniture and other stuff, but Bob noticed that Jason seemed to light up with smiles and giggles every time someone would approach him. Ben, on the other hand, seemed to be oblivious to everything. He simply stared up at the leaves on the trees. Jason had a toy in his hand and was constantly chewing it or looking at it, or shaking it. Ben's hands lay quietly in his lap. Bob noticed these things, but in the frenzy of the sale, preparing to move, watching our two daughters, these observations slipped into the back of our minds. Later, we would return to this event and realize that we had been witnessing the early signs of what we now knew was Ben's autism.

Another characteristic we began to see was that Ben didn't "play" the same way his peers of the same age did. We began to notice a lack of responsiveness when we tried to cuddle him. His facial expressions were flat, stoic. His body postures were odd, different from what we had experienced with our daughters. When we would pick Ben up, his body was limp.

"He feels like a rag doll, a really heavy one." I commented. He didn't tense up in anticipation of being lifted. He just hung there in my arms.

He did not automatically smile or reach his arms or legs around us. We would hug him and coo into his ear, but he rarely seemed to acknowledge our interactions. He seemed to look through us, never at us. He didn't smile or respond much to us. He didn't babble or make any baby-like sounds

"How could we not notice these things?" we asked ourselves later, beating ourselves up for being so unobservant, but we just didn't. Did we ignore these things? I don't know. I think we just didn't see them, we didn't notice. We just saw Ben as normal, just as we saw our daughters. We did what we thought was right by doing what we thought they needed. Our lives were busy and we probably made excuses. We excused his slow development by reminding ourselves that he had been quite heavy at birth (9 lb. 10 oz). By the time we adopted him four months later he was close to 20 pounds. Because he had been in foster care, too, we fell into blaming his foster family for not stimulating him by playing with him. We had no evidence for this. It just seemed logical to us.

When Ben was around two, however, we could not avoid noticing that he did not do the same things our other daughters had done at the same age. He seemed content to simply sit in his infant seat or lie in the playpen. He made little effort to sit up. If we sat him up he would stay in that position. If we laid him on his back or his stomach he would remain in that position. He didn't try pulling himself up to a standing position, and seemed to have no interest in crawling or walking unless we helped him. He didn't seek out toys to play with. If we put a toy in his hand, he would hold onto it until he dropped it, but then would not search for it. His favorite position was on his back, with his legs extended up in the air and then he would flip his fingers in front of his face. He didn't seem to notice his sisters or us moving around him. He was totally content to "stay in his own little world." For a while, we thought he was lazy. We expected him to grow out of it. Penny had been aloof when she came to live with us too, but she outgrew it and became active. Surely, Ben would too.

••

A story – We're not making fun of him.

One of Ben's favorite ways to entertain himself when he was a toddler was to lie on his back and extend his legs in the air wiggling his toes toward the ceiling while flapping his hands in front of his face. As an infant this activity hadn't looked so unusual, but now, as a two and a half year old, he looked bizarre.

One afternoon I walked into our playroom to find all three of my kids laying on their backs wiggling their hands and their feet in the air.

"Stop making fun of Ben!" I reprimanded Sherry and Penny. They immediately stopped but looked stunned.

"But Mom, we were playing with him. We weren't making fun of him. You're always telling us to play with him, so we were. He likes to do this."

I was chagrined. "Oops, sorry," I said lamely and quietly left the room.

••

As we reflect on these early years we realize that even now, at different times in his daily life, Ben exhibits all the classic characteristics of autism as described in the professional literature (i.e. DSM-IV manual (2000). Within the spectrum of autistic disorders, he fits quite naturally near the most complicated end. His social skills are poor. He can say "hi" when prompted, but rarely greets people spontaneously. Generally, Ben doesn't make eye contact, unless he really wants you to do something or respond to him. His verbal communication is pretty limited and sometimes bizarre. One of his favorite spoken phrases for the longest time was "pull the ends." It took us years to discover that he was trying to warn us that he was losing control and would soon start scratching himself and us.

"Impaired communication," that's professional "speak" meaning the kid doesn't talk or communicate like the rest of his or her peers. By the time Ben was three years old he drove us all crazy with his repetitive "wanna go to McDonald's, wanna go to McDonald's, wanna go to McDonald's". He would repeat this phrase ad nauseum. Of course we took him to McDonald's, but not nearly as frequently as he asked. His idiosyncratic "pull the ends" was even more frustrating because it made no sense to us. Rarely did Ben initiate language, but would repeat what he heard in the same tone of voice. We thought, at times, that Ben's random verbalizations were only meant to drive us nuts. Later we realized that he was trying to tell us something in the only way he knew how. Once we understood this, we tried harder to "make sense" of his "jibber jabber" as we called it.

Routines and consistency

Ben never seemed to need routines or consistency, which, we learned later, many other individuals with autism crave. We have often described our life as chaotic and have jokingly said that the consistency in Ben's life is chaos. Maybe that is why he always seemed pretty flexible. Of course, we always tried to plan thoughtfully for each of our children so they were curious, not stressed and resentful. For some children, however, a change in routines can be emotionally and behaviorally devastating. Most often Ben was content to listen to music, play with water, or eat. He still enjoys these pastimes. Why would we deny him these? However, if he became obsessive or unable to stop, we helped him to move on to something else. Sometimes we were not successful, but we never assumed he should be prevented from doing what he wanted and needed. Routines and predictability are important for all of us; they connote safety.

Today, these characteristics and others that Ben engaged in would have been clear indicators of autism, but this was the early 1970s. Autism was rare then, 1 in

10,000 or so and very little was understood about this complicated disorder. Bob and I certainly didn't know very much, although we tried to read everything we could find. Professionals, such as psychologists and psychiatrists, even some teacher and school administrators, believed that the bizarre behaviors that some children like Ben engaged in were indicative of Childhood Schizophrenia. Ben and other children like him were considered emotionally disturbed, moderately to severely cognitively impaired (i.e. retarded), and functionally incapable of learning. Perhaps they could be trained to do simple tasks, but their future was bleak. Fortunately, today's professionals have more information, training and research that enlighten their understanding of this complex disorder. Indeed, parents have become zealots about learning about autism and their legal rights. They have become knowledgeable and sophisticated advocates for their child, and they have learned the importance of working cooperatively together. Bob and I hoped that we contributed in some way to this awakening. Actually, we didn't understand all of this until later. Right now, we had to figure out what we should do.

Could it be autism?

By the time Ben was three we had heard both Ms. Patrick and the evaluation center team suggest "autism", but we didn't know what it was. Bob began researching autism, going to the college library searching through the relevant professional journals. It didn't take him long to see that we might be heading in the right direction. One night he handed me an article describing the common characteristics believed to be associated with autism.

"Sue, it's like the author of this article is describing Ben. Everything he lists fits Ben. You have to read this. You have to read this now." I could hear the urgency in his voice.

What do we do now?

About the same time, our local school district was trying to "find" children with special needs as part of their compliance with P.L. 94-142, the Education for All Handicapped Children's Act (now known as IDEA). A variety of venues were used, including public service announcements on radio and television, and brightly colored fliers in pediatricians' offices and health care clinics. School personnel were alerted to identify children who might need special education services. As part of New York State's Child Find initiative, public service announcements were broadcast on the television where the announcer said something like "if you think your child might be handicapped, call this number". I called the next morning.

"Hello, This is the New York State Child Find Hotline. We are trying to identify children who might be handicapped. Do you think your child is handicapped?" It seemed such a simple question, but it was the first time I had thought of Ben in this way, as a possibility, a reality? I remembered Penny's question about Ben being normal, but I had always just thought of him as Ben. Now, I was being asked to possibly see a different Ben.

"I'm not sure," I continued, my voice soft, tentative, flat.

"He is in a special preschool program for handicapped children run by our local BOCES (Board of Cooperative Educational Services), but we really don't know what is wrong with him."

I hated that word "wrong". It sounded so pejorative. It brought back memories of when the surrendering adoption agency worker had offered to take Ben back, as if he was a damaged and needed to be traded in for something better. I felt weird telling this stranger on the phone that Ben might he handicapped, but I wanted information and help. I told her what I knew, that Ben was 3 years old, didn't speak although he occasionally made sounds, was barely toilet trained, didn't seem to play with toys like our two older children had, seemed to be aloof and distant from the rest of us, occasionally he flapped his hands in front of his eyes/face, and, generally, he was quite content to be by himself. I also mentioned that his teacher and the findings from the evaluation center had both suggested that he might have some characteristics of autism.

"I really don't know what this is – this autism stuff."

I don't remember the exact questions she asked me, but eventually she said, "I think you need to talk to Hillery Schneiderman. She is a parent of an autistic son and she works at the Early Childhood Direction Center at the Center on Human Policy at Syracuse University.

This was too much information for me at first. I was happy, however, to know of another parent with whom I could talk. I called her.

It was a brief, but friendly chat. She asked me if I knew about the Jowonio School in Syracuse, and when I said that I didn't., she briefly described the school.

"Peter Knoblock and Ellen Barnes, they're the directors, and they are very knowledgeable about children with emotional disturbances and autism. It's a very good school for handicapped children and normal, or typical, children as well. Tell them I recommended you call. I am sure they can help you and your son."

I thanked Mrs. Schneiderman, but then I hesitated. I was scared. Calling meant that I was publicly admitting that my child was truly handicapped. I wasn't sure I was ready to admit this even to myself, but I also knew that what ever I could do to help Ben was the right thing. It was worth the try.

Chapter 7

Jowonio – Our introduction to inclusion

As I dialed Jowonio's phone number, I remembered Mrs. Schneiderman describing the staff and directors.

"These are good people. The school's name, well, that's an Indian word meaning "to set free." She continued, " Jowonio is sort of like a free school in that they believe that all children can learn."

I liked that. Sherry and Penny had attended a free school when they were younger, and had developed into hungry learners. This was what I wanted for Ben, too.

When I did call, the person who answered the phone was quite friendly and invited us to visit.

"Be sure to bring Ben." Her voice was warm and reassuring.

I am not sure what I expected at that first meeting, but after some of our previous encounters with professionals I certainly was not prepared to be so warmly welcomed. I guess I thought we would find some sort of clinical evaluation setting like before, but instead we were settled into the school's Main Office. It was a large room with comfortable well-worn chairs and a sofa. We were offered coffee and Ben was offered some juice and cookies. As we settled in I looked around the room. There were boxes of materials at one end, lots of books and some filing cabinets, and a conference table and chairs. We quickly realized that this room served multiple purposes. It looked a bit weathered around the edges, but it was also homey.

The co-directors, Ellen Barnes and Peter Knoblock, welcomed us and invited us to sit down while Ben wandered around the room. I felt comfortable and began to relax. They asked questions, but didn't probe or make us feel like we were on the spot. They watched Ben and our interactions with him. They asked us to describe Ben, his development, and our family. As we talked, they occasionally asked a question.

"What was he like as a baby? When did Ben begin to walk? What does he enjoy? How does he fit in with his sisters?"

They weren't interrogating us, just asking questions. They seemed genuinely interested. It made me feel good that neither of them held a clipboard or a file folder. They didn't write anything down which put me at ease. too. This was a discussion,

Beautiful Ben

not an interview. They often nodded and smiled as we told them stories about Ben and our family. Occasionally, one of them got up and went over to Ben, offering a cookie or a toy. I think something was said to him, but I couldn't hear it. He seemed perfectly at home.

After a while, Ellen asked, "Would you like me to tell you about Jowonio?" We were all ears. Together, they told us about their approach to education.

"We believe in a developmental approach," Ellen said.

"We start where each child is, and build on what he or she can do, introducing new concepts and skills based upon what each child is ready for. We challenge with support, but don't push without it."

"What do you mean 'with support'?" I asked.

Ellen explained how each of the teachers was trained to give individualized encouragement along with physical, emotional, and/or social guidance to enable each child to work toward achieving specific goals. She added that having other children who did not have any problems or handicaps, in the same classroom was fostered friendships and provided good role models. It was more than I could understand. I kept picturing the group activities in Ms. Patrick's room. Ellen suggested that while Peter and his assistant, Cindy (a doctoral student in special education at Syracuse University) took Ben for a more in depth evaluation, she could show Bob and I several classrooms where what she was describing was being implemented. We agreed.

"When we are finished, we can come back here and talk some more." I liked that we were not being rushed or pressured. Intuitively, we knew that Ben would be safe with Peter. He was a gentle man who briefly described that he and Cindy would invite Ben to play with them. It sounded so non-threatening. We wanted to watch, but Ellen reassured us that Ben would be better without looking to us for direction.

Seeing inclusion and support - first hand

In each of the classrooms that we visited we found a vibrant atmosphere where ten to twelve 3 and 4, or 4 and 5 year old children, were playing with different materials. Ellen explained how each room had different stations or centers that contained specific toys and items that were meant to engage the children in exploration of their different senses. In the first room we visited I was immediately drawn to the "water table". It was about 10 inches deep with about 4 inches of water in it. Four or five children were around the edges of the tables, sleeves pushed up, plastic aprons on, and their hands immersed in the water. The teacher was encouraging the children to drop different toys into the water.

"Oh look, Mandy, that ball floats. How about your toy car, Angel, do you think that will float too?"

Angel looked at the little matchbox car and then at Mandy's plastic floating ball. She looked quizzical and gave a little shrug. She said something but I couldn't understand it.

"Well, I don't know either." The teacher continued.

"Shall we drop it in and see what happens?"

Angel quickly pulled the little car closer to her chest and covered it with her other hand. It was clear to me that she was not about to drop her car into the water. I wondered what would happen.

"Conrad, what do you think? Will Angel's car sink or float."

"Oh, I know. It'll sink!" Conrad beamed.

Angel looked dubious. The teacher got another car from the toy bin at the end of the table.

"Conrad, can you drop this into the water so we can see what happens?"

Still smiling excitedly, Conrad took the car and with great fanfare, extended his arm out over the water.

"Watch, Angel. Watch what happens."

He let go of the car. With a splash the little car hit the surface of the water and plunged to the bottom.

"It sinked." Conrad jumped up and down.

"See Angel. It sinked. It did." He was pointing at the small car submerged in the water. He was grinning and looking from the car to Angel.

The teacher smiled at him.

"Yes, Conrad, it did sink. Mandy's ball floats on the top, but your car sank to the bottom. Can you find it?"

Conrad was up for the challenge and quickly plunged his hands into the water. Within seconds his dripping hands displayed his car.

"Here it is!" He was almost shouting with excitement.

"Angel, you could try that with your car, too."

Angel had watched all of this, but it I could see that Angel was not going to let go of her car. The teacher smiled.

"Maybe you would like to try a different toy."

She offered Angel a little plastic circle. Tentatively, Angel took the circle and carefully dropped it into the water.

"It floats, just like my ball," said Mandy, pleased with her discovery.

Angel watched with wide eyes, still clinging to her little car.

I moved to the next center where children were building with blocks. There were 5-6 children here, but they were all working on trying to build together. There were children putting blocks together to make towers and others who were making squares and rectangles. No teacher was with them. There wasn't much conversation, just building. One child was not really participating, just watching when one of the boys handed him a block.

"Here, you can have this one."

The child took the block and then added it to the tower. It immediately fell over and everyone laughed.

"Do it again, Jake." Said one little girl as she clapped her hands and jumped up and down.

In another area I saw children playing dress up. It looked like they were pretending to go shopping. One little girl held a pocket book and was asking to buy some fruit. On the counter in front of her was a display of different plastic foods.

"Do you want a banana?" Asked the little boy with the apron on, and he held out a plastic banana.

"That will cost $7.00, and he expectantly held out is hand. The little girl began rummaging in her purse. I smiled and moved on to the next center.

At each center I visited the children were engaged in play with each other. I began to notice that some of the children reminded me of Ben. They were not as engaged, standing on the edge of the activity. I looked back at Angel, still holding her little car, and realized that she might be one of the handicapped children Ellen had said were part of each class.

"Would Ben fit in here?" I wondered to myself.

As I studied the rooms more carefully, I began to realize that the adults were moving among the children talking and playing with them. In one room, a little girl had leg braces on and thick glasses. She sat in a little chair at a table with other children who were drawing with chunky chalk. The teacher was sitting next to her, helping her hold onto the chalk. Ellen explained that Cherie had cerebral palsy and one of her physical therapy goals was to develop her grasping and pincer skills.

"Here at Jowonio we try to embed these specialized goals into routine play activities, and we try to make it a social experience with peers. We believe that children learn a lot from each other and they can model for each other what to do. Of course, for more intensive therapies, we may have the child go to the Kaleidoscope room. There a trained physical or occupational therapist can engage the child in prescribed interventions. Usually we ask the child to bring along one or two friends from the class to participate with them. That way the typical, non- handicapped child, won't be afraid of the handicapped child or the specialized equipment that may be needed. It's more fun that way, too," she added.

Back to the Main Office and Ben

It was time for us to go back to the Main Office and rejoin Ben and Peter. As we approached the office Ben was walking down the hall holding Peter's hand and smiling. It was a beautiful picture. Bob and I smiled at each other. We knew this was where we wanted Ben to go to school. First, however, we wanted to hear what Peter had to say about Ben.

We settled into the comfortable sofa. Ben seemed content to continue to explore the office, especially the heaters that extended along the outside wall under the windows. Air was puffing out and he seemed engaged in putting his hand over the vents and then pulling them back. I wondered what he was thinking, but then I heard Peter begin to speak.

"Well, Ben is quite a fascinating little boy," he began.

"Cindy and I played with him and we agreed that Ben has all the characteristics associated with Classical Autism. In fact, we think that Ben could author a book on autism."

What a positive statement. It took the edge off the despair that we might have felt hearing this diagnosis. Peter smiled and waited for us to digest this news before he continued.

"I think Ben would do very well here at Jowonio. We could help him develop his language and social skills. I think he would like it here. He is an engaging child. He will win friends quickly, and we will help him learn how to do that and more."

Peter paused, then looked at Ben. We all did. Then he continued.

"We also can offer support to you as parents. You can meet other parents here and learn strategies from them to help Ben progress. We would welcome you all here, anytime."

Ben enters Jowonio

The year was 1978. Ben entered Jowonio that fall. That summer, before school began, we moved to a small rural community. Our house sat on the edge of a small lake, where we spent hours swimming, fishing and canoeing,

I contacted the local school district to inquire about the process for having Ben officially attend Jowonio in the fall. Because he had been attending a "special preschool program for handicapped children" before we moved, the school requested a copy of his Individualized Educational Plan (IEP). This was a mandated educational plan required as part of the new law, P.L. 94-142, that identified his deficits, educational goals, and appropriate therapies. I knew about this law and saw how it could potentially benefit Ben.

The IEP prepared by Ms. Patrick and her therapy staff in the handicapped preschool classroom was supposed to reflect his current levels of skill in different areas, and it was supposed to set personal goals for him to achieve in the next academic setting. What we received, however, made no sense to us. His IEP was one page long as follows:

Ben's " Present Level of Achievement" was listed as follows:

1.   Denver Developmental Screening Test

Personal-Social skills: 4-9

Fine-Motor Adaptive Skills: 3-3

Language Skills: 4-0

Gross Motor Skills: 4-3

2.   Portage Guide to Early Education Checklist –

Skills at:	0-1	1-2	2-3	3-4	4-5	5-6
Socialization	96%	100%	88%	33%	22%	0%
Language	100%	78%	50%	8%	0	0
Self-help	100%	100%	100%	80%	21%	0
Cognitive	100%	90%	75%	21%	0	0
Motor	100%	100%	82%	93%	31%	3%

3.   Preschool Language Scale

Auditory Comprehension Age: 30 months

Verbal Ability Age: 34.4 months

Total age: 32.25 months

Sue Lehr

The rest of the IEP detailed Ben's placement in the self contained preschool classroom for the full day, the names of the assessments used to determine his deficits, and the extent to which he should receive speech/language therapy. The IEP recommended that Ben be placed in the Emotionally Disturbed Classroom on the main BOCES campus in Crown City. Honest, that is what they called the room.

"So, the room makes you emotionally disturbed?" I knew this was silly, but also very scary. For us as new parents, the percentages were both meaningless and frightening. Because of Bob's training in psychology, we could make some sense of what these scores meant. We didn't understand how the scores on different tests were reflected in the goals set for Ben. Nor did we understand how the classroom teacher would teach these. The thing that had bothered us the most, however, was there was no description of who Ben was as a person, a whole person. It totally lacked any values.

Until we met with Peter, we had only these evaluation results and the recommendation that Ben go on to the ED classroom at BOCES. The school officials in Crown City had based this on the results of testing done by the school psychologist. I remembered that testing. It was gruesome.

The first time Ben had been tested by the school psychologist had not gone well. Ben would not respond to the tasks she set out for him. He became irritable and uncooperative.

"This is not going well. I am going to discontinue the session and reschedule for another time when I will attempt to test him again. If necessary I may try some reinforcements, such as tokens, you know, giving him a small toy to play with." I knew intuitively that this new session would end in failure too. Ben simply wasn't interested in toys. Besides the psychologist explained that this reinforcement would contaminate her data, which meant it was basically a waste of her time.

"And mine too." I thought this, but didn't say anything. I wanted Ben to shine, but I was realistic enough to realize he was not going to comply with her demands to build block towers, or draw pictures of people. At the conclusion of the second session of testing, also abandoned because Ben was uncooperative, she informed Bob and me that her diagnosis was Childhood Schizophrenia. She said this with such finality in her voice that I felt Ben had just been issued his death sentence.

"First he was brain damaged, now he is Schizophrenic. What's next? Good God, the poor kid is only three years old."

Beautiful Ben

We had read that autism might be a subset condition of Childhood Schizophrenia, but because there was so little known about it at the time, this was not acceptable as a legitimate diagnosis by professional psychiatrists or psychologists. Schizophrenia sounded so scary to us. We didn't believe he was crazy and we certainly didn't want him to go into a classroom of emotionally disturbed kids.

The teacher for this Emotionally Disturbed classroom was a friend of mine. I had visited her classroom, however, and was horrified with what she had to do. Her students were tough to teach, disturbed and emotionally fragile. She had very little help in the room, and the resources were mediocre at best. Even though she was my friend, I told her, "Linda, I can't have Ben here. I just can't. He's not like those kids." I remember how she looked at me with such sadness and pity in her eyes. If she had spoken at that moment, I think she probably would have shaken her head in despair and said "You poor misguided fool." I was so glad we moved away. Jowonio gave me hope.

Bob and I met with the members of the Waters School District Committee on the Handicapped (COH) who received all of Ben's preschool records along with the recommendations and conclusions of their psychologist. At first, they assumed they would simply have to make a referral to BOCES and then arrange for Ben's transportation. We understood how they could think this, but then informed them of what had happened when Ben had visited and been evaluated at Jowonio. They agreed to send for these records. We were encouraged. It didn't take long for the principal of Waters Elementary School, who was also the Chair Person of the COH, to formally recommend that Ben attend Jowonio. He had visited the school along with another member of the committee and was favorably impressed. Although he had only briefly met Ben, he recommended to the committee that they approve this new placement, which they did.

It didn't take us long to realize that sending Ben to Jowonio was one of the best things we ever did for him or for us. It was here that we learned to see Ben as a whole child and to recognize that his disability was only one part of him. Here was a school staffed with caring, knowledgeable and well-trained individuals who knew how to value Ben for what he could do. Even more they knew how to engage him in practical experiences that built new social, emotional, language and behavioral skills. It was every parent's dream come true, but at the time we did not fully appreciate what was happening for Ben or us.

Ben's life at Jowonio

Ben's first teacher at Jowonio, Valerie, was a gentle, soft-spoken, incredibly skilled teacher. It seemed that teaching came naturally to Valerie, but we learned that she worked very hard at her craft. She showed Ben how to have fun with learning. She planned every interaction and activity. She thought long and hard about what was best for Ben and his progress as she planned. She invited him into exploring new environments and exposed him to new experiences. Through careful observations of Ben and the other students as they interacted with him, she learned what kind of support Ben needed to be successful. She also learned, quite quickly, what was not going to work. She talked frequently with us, asking for ideas, problem solving, making suggestions for things we could do to follow up lessons she taught. She listened to Ben intently; not just to his limited speech, but to the myriad ways in which he communicated what he was thinking and feeling. She noted when he would start rocking, flapping his hands, smiled or laughed, or when he moved away or cried. She observed what was happening and what occurred later, always trying to determine what Ben wanted, needed, or was trying to express. We welcomed her into our home, and she visited often. Ben became attached to Valerie; we all did.

I think every parent is afraid of what might happen to his or her child, especially when Mommy or Daddy cannot be there. For parents of children with disabilities, especially those with limited communication skills, sending your child off to school can be frightening. There is the constant fear that others will not understand your child, or will not treat him or her the way you do. All parents live in dread that something harmful will happen to their child whether it is an injury, an emotional hurt (e.g. teasing, ridicule, bullying) or just feeling isolated, alone and friendless.

Recognizing segregation won't help Ben

Being in Valerie's class solidified our feelings about how important it was for him to among his peers, and especially those without disabilities. He was happy there, and he was liked by the kids and the staff. Periodically, we began to think about Ben's future. Could Ben learn to be independent and resourceful? Could he make friends? Would he ever date, get married, have a career? We also worried about what would happen to Ben when we died, and what if that happened unexpectedly. Who would be there for Ben? What would happen to him? It would have been easy, very easy, to ignore these questions. It was very, very tempting.

"What if we die tomorrow?" I was thinking of my aunt and uncle who had been killed in a car accident when their daughter was only five years old. They didn't expect something like this to happen. No one did. There were no wills. I didn't want what happened to my cousin to happen to Ben.

"We are going to have to seriously think about this and make decisions about what we think is best for Ben and the girls. We shouldn't let this get lost. It is too important." One of the first things we did was make out Wills, specifying exactly what would happen to Sherry, Penny and Ben in the event we died unexpectedly. It was small comfort, but it was a beginning.

You want to do what?

Meanwhile, Ben was heading off each day to Jowonio and we became increasingly confident that he was progressing. Of course we worried, but we knew he was safe, even when Valerie announced that the class was going camping. Ben had never spent the night away from us. He had gone camping before, but this was entirely different. She wanted to take the kids to a nearby forest - in January?

"You have got to be kidding!" I was trying to restrain my voice and my fear.

"No. We will plan well. It will really be fun. We're going to invite the families for a potluck dinner the last night. The kids are quite excited."

She had already told the students about the camping trip. I didn't see anyway of backing out. If we didn't let Ben go, how would he feel? What message would we be sending to the other kids? It didn't make any difference. I was terrified.

"Bob, what do you think of this? Ben might..." I got lost in my thoughts, envisioning all sorts of scenarios.

"He might - what? Get lost, get hurt, not like the experience? All of these are possible, maybe even probable, but......." he paused and I waited.

"I think we have to let him try. Valerie seems to think he will be okay and I also think we have to trust her."

Valerie assured us that if any problem arose, she would be sure to call us from the Ranger's station. She also explained to us, and to all the other nervous parents, that she had designed a schedule so that every child was assigned to a staff person at all times. That person would be responsible for making sure the child was safe, engaged, and having fun. This schedule was revised slightly for each night so that different staff were awake for a two-hour period and were expected to keep track of the children assigned to their "watch". It seemed like she had thought of everything, but I was still scared.

It was hard to tell how Ben felt about the trip. He seemed happy, but I really didn't know what he understood or expected. I packed his duffle bag, rolled his sleeping bag, tied on his pillow, and packed his snow pants, mittens and heavy boots. All the while, I was terrified, but also excited. This was Ben's first adventure on his own, with his friends and his teachers. I had to believe he would be okay.

They left from school in the early afternoon, got to the site and set up their camp. At least, that was the plan, as we knew it. Bob and I waited at home. I think we both expected the phone to ring, but it never did. They stayed for two nights. On the last night, we went to the potluck dinner. Everyone looked a bit scraggly, dirty around the edges, but generally in good spirits. Ben was busy with Kerry, a teaching assistant, and two other kids. They were helping to get the dinner ready. I had so many questions, as did the other parents, but we watched and listened as the kids told us about their adventure. The kids had learned how to plan meals, share in the work, play in the snow, sleep in bunks, sing songs, be safe around the campfire and keep warm. As we shared our meal and sat around the final bonfire there was a group sing along. Ben hardly noticed we were there. He was too busy. Kerry told us how she had helped Ben get to sleep each night by singing songs. The other kids in the cabin loved this too. She said she had a great time and really enjoyed being with Ben. Years later Kerry adopted her own daughter with severe disabilities. They visit us each summer.

The school year resumed after the holidays and Valerie talked at length about what we could do to reinforce what she was teaching. She invited us into the classroom and welcomed our participation. She made us feel that we were part of a team along with the speech therapist, physical and occupational therapists, and the assistant teachers.

Her attitude was "We are all in this together, for the kids."

Behaviorism, Applied Behavioral Analysis, and what is best for Ben…

When Ben entered Jowonio, Bob had been teaching at SUNY Cortland in the Psychology Department for over ten years. He taught courses in Learning, General Psychology, and Motivation. At the time, behaviorism was emerging within Psychology as the new area of research. Bob had been trained in experimental psychology so behaviorism was not new to him. Now however, it was being applied in the school setting, especially with children like Ben who exhibited behavioral and/or emotional problems.

Along with two colleagues Bob developed a new course, Behavior Modification, which the three professors team-taught. Bob considered the basic principals of behaviorism to be valid; keep data so you know what is happening, be consistent with your protocol of interventions, use reinforcement to increase the frequency of the correct response, use punishment to extinguish responses that are negative.

Before sending Ben to Jowonio we had used behavior modification. His language was really delayed so, along with the wife of one of Bob's psychology colleagues, he introduced Ben to a language acquisition program. Ben would sit on a little chair in a clinic room. Jane, a social worker, would sit facing Ben. She held a spoon with a little dab of sweetened instant tea – one of Ben's favorite tastes.

"Ben, say 'at'."

She would wait for a response. If Ben made any sound that was close to this, she would give him a taste of the tea and say, "Good boy, Ben". Then she would sit him back down in his chair and move to the next word on the list for that session. Each session lasted twenty minutes. She would repeat these sessions two or three times each day.

Bob and I would do these at home too. Sometimes we blew bubbles for the reinforcement or we would clap our hands and jump up and down and shout "Hooray for Ben." What ever worked. Sometimes Ben made sounds or even said the targeted word, and sometimes he didn't. On those unsuccessful trials, he didn't get any reinforcement.

At Jowonio, however, we didn't see these clinical behavioral interventions being used. Instead, Ben's language goals were embedded into his play activities.

"Here Ben, this is a baseball bat, a bat.

What is it called? Please give the bat to Eugene.

Can you say, 'Here is the bat.'?

Ben would be encouraged to say "bat" while he was handing the bat to Eugene.

"Jowonio changed me from a strict behaviorist to a person who could see the whole child. " Bob said matter-of-factly.

"The principles of behavior modification are good, but you can't treat a child as a thing to be manipulated. If you do that, you take away his or her humanity. I began to consider the parallels with our adopted daughter, Penny. She is multiracial and has dark skin. Does that mean I should treat her differently? Does that mean I should manipulate her as if she isn't really a person? Why should her skin color change things? Why should Ben's autism mean I should treat him differently? Penny and Ben are human beings, not simple organisms to be managed. Sherry used to tell us 'I am my own little person.' Yes, she is, and so is every child. Each is unique and deserves to be valued as such. Behavior modification may work for rats and other laboratory animals, but Ben is my child. He is not an animal."

Over time, we would repeatedly return to this discussion of racial issues, oppression, segregation, punishment, discrimination based on disability, gender and/ or race. We would reflect on how these mirrored what was happening to Ben.

Ben attended Jowonio for two years. We had hoped that he would stay there through his entire school career, but the governing board of Jowonio had decided to focus on the needs of preschool children and discontinue the upper grades. We informed our home school district that Ben would enter kindergarten when he graduated from Jowonio at the ripe old age of five. With the school administration we used these two years to plan and get ready. We worked as a team with the elementary principal and the superintendent. Periodically we met with the members of the Committee on the Handicapped (as it was called then) to up date them on what Ben was doing and what needs he would present when he entered kindergarten. The principal visited Jowonio on several occasions. Everything seemed to be going smoothly.

Reflections

We learned so much from our experiences at Jowonio. Probably the most important thing we learned was that Ben did not have to be defined by his autism. Yes, it was a part of him that he was going to have to manage, we all were, but it wasn't the most important thing about him. He could learn things, too. It was exciting to witness this happening. He could develop friendships with his peers, and enjoy some of the same activities. From watching his teachers and other staff, we began to recognize what makes good teachers; it is not just their training and professional skill, but also revolves around the positive values they have that expect all children to learn. We learned the value of teamwork where everyone, including us, contributed what they could without regard for professional titles or responsibilities. And finally, we celebrated the notion that this stuff of learning is all about the kids and what they need and want. In this way, we all will continue to grow and, indeed, the world will be a better place.

Chapter 8

Summer vacation - a time for different fun things

Summer came and once again we relished living on our little lake. The kids would ride their bikes, fish, swim and play. The "summer folk" would return to their camps and everyone would reunite at the Main Dock. This was a dock about mid way down our dead end road. It had a sliding board, diving board, and a paid lifeguard on duty. Usually the lifeguard was one of the older kids from the street who had been certified through the Red Cross Water Safety training program. The adults on the street all were members of the lake's Park Association and part of our dues were used to pay the lifeguard. The kids formed their own Junior Association. They organized movie nights on Friday. The Juniors also were in charge of several annual events – the Girls overnight and the Boys overnight. The older teens would supervise the younger kids on an overnight camping trip on the local mountain. Of course, the boys always raided the girls, and vice versa, but everyone had fun.

We loved the summer. We made sure that Ben was at the Main Dock swimming with the other kids. We wanted him to be part of this community as much as any other child. The big event near the end of summer was Carnival. This was a whole family affair that centered on a theme chosen by the Juniors. The day would start with a parade, sometimes on the street and sometimes in boats out on the lake. Each camp could dress in costumes, build a float, and vie for winning a ribbon. Our family and the family next door, the Fudges, always entered together. We would usually begin the evening before carnival sitting on the Fudge's porch sharing a bottle of wine (or more) and shouting out ideas of how we would dress or depict the theme. We felt a kinship with the Fudges because their son, Gerard (who was Ben's age) had been diagnosed with Hydrocephalus about the same time Ben was diagnosed with autism. It was a parent-to-parent connection. We needed each other.

Carnival's Tacky Award goes to the Fudge/Lehr Camps

Having and maintaining a sense of humor held us together along with deep discussions about the future for our children. Parents of kids like Ben and Gerard can live in such despair, but humor always brought us back in balance. Often others, outside the "parents" experience couldn't really understand how we felt, but we needed a release; a way of laughing that defused the tensions and allowed us to carry on.

One Carnival, the Fudge/Lehr land "float" was almost kicked out of the parade. The theme was Holidays. After undoubtedly too much wine, we decided to "play" on the idea of Labor Day. Our neighbor, Emily, and I dressed up as very pregnant women. We took the top off of our Jeep and fastened a piece of 4' x 8' plywood across the back seat. Russell, Emily's husband, carried a sign that said, "Doctor?" Gerard, their son, wore a sign that said "Dad" and carried bubble gum cigars that he handed out to the people standing along the street. Alexander, Gerard's best friend who often spent summers here, courageously dressed up as a brightly colored stork, beak and all, and perched himself on the front of the Jeep. We decorated the car to look like a Red Cross ambulance. Bob drove and Ben sat in the passenger seat dressed as a nurse. Penny and Rachel, Emily and Russell's daughter, dressed as babies and hid under the plywood platform. We carried a sign that read "Labor Day????" As Bob drove the Jeep in the parade, Emily and I would cry out "Who is the father?" And then Penny and Rachel would pop up and cry like newborns. We all were laughing so hard, but we were not so sure the rest of our neighbors thought it was a funny as we did. We didn't win any prize that year, but we thoroughly enjoyed ourselves.

Another year, the theme was music. It was a boat parade, so we sat Ben in our rowboat with his piano keyboard across his lap. We dressed him as Michael Jackson, white glove and all. We set up a tape recorder and blared "Thriller" music as we passed by the judge's stand. We were a hit.

With each theme we would think of how to make it work for Ben. One year, when the theme was Disney hits, he was Winnie the Pooh. We filled an old cookie jar with animal crackers, painted it gold, and wrote "honey" on the outside. Bob dressed as Tigger in long underwear that I had spray-painted orange with black stripes, and he sported a long tail that trailed down the street. Ben was happy to walk along, munching on his animal crackers as "Tigger" danced along with him. The rest of us wore costumes too, to fit the theme, but Bob and Ben were the stars.

As the years went by we became more sophisticated in our depiction of the theme. Our best year, the one were we won first prize; the theme was "Books". We really outdid ourselves with that one. Ben was about 20 and now lived with his friends Jesse and Jenn. They had joined our growing family and were up for the idea of carnival. As usual we did a "play" on words. We covered Jesse in hairy material, gave him a golf club, and with his shoulder length long hair, he became "Hairy Putter." Bob, with his snow white long beard and shoulder length white hair wore a long black silky robe and went as the "Lord of the Rings". It was Ben, however, who stole the show and guaranteed us a first prize. Several weeks before Carnival he

Beautiful Ben

had broken his heel jumping off a stage at a local park. Although he didn't have a cast, his foot was swollen and he was supposed to stay off it. He dressed as "The English Patient" sporting a World War I army hat (it had belonged to Bob's Dad) and we bandaged him from head to toe. He rode in Grandad's wheel chair with Jenn, dressed as his nurse, pushing him. He was "The English Patient" to a T.

Ben loves the lake and swimming so summers went smoothly and were fun. Each summer ended with Carnival. As a family, we would always participate in the parade, supporting Sherry and Penny in the swimming events, attending the potluck dinner and making sure the girls got to go to the square dance at the end of the day. We made sure Ben was with us, but we never let him enter the Carnival water races. These were events like the boys' or girls' doggie paddle, the cannonball contest, the beginner's diving contest, an egg and spoon race (swimming while holding a spoon in your mouth with an egg cradled in it - "if you drop it, go get it and carry on), or the peanut race for toddlers (capturing peanuts in their mouths - "no hands, please"). It was a friendly and fun time. Parents and grandparents cheered and proudly wore the ribbons their children had won. It was a community event and every one participated, well almost everyone.

· ·

A story - And the children shall lead us.

There was a knock on our back door. I opened it to find about 6 of the neighborhood kids, all around Ben's age standing there.

"Mrs. Lehr, we all have been talking about Carnival." I assumed they were going to ask me to sign up for what I would make for the community dinner. I was well known for my vegetable lasagna, so I felt a bit smug. I had already made it and had stored it in my freezer. But that wasn't what they were here about. They had more serious thoughts on their minds.

"We think you should let Ben be in the swimming races." I was stunned.

Ben was about 8 or 9 at the time. The swimming races at Carnival started with the Peanut Race for children up to age 3. Each event was for different aged children so that the competition is fair. We had never let Ben participate because we didn't want him to get in the way of the other children. I guess we thought we were protecting them, or were we really trying to over protect Ben? Right now, however, what I thought didn't make any difference. These kids had decided that Ben would participate. They wanted him to sign up for the Junior Doggie Paddle and they had figured out how to help him "train" for it. For the rest of the summer leading up to Carnival, these kids, including Ben's two sisters, practiced with him.

Carnival arrived and the water events began. As the Junior Doggie Paddle event approached I felt myself getting nervous. Penny and Sherry, along with several other kids, came and got Ben. They took him to sign in at the judges' table and then showed him where to stand on the dock. Ben was smiling. Sherry stood next to Ben. Penny jumped in the water and swam to the finish line.

She clambered out of the water and yelled, "Here I am Ben." Several of the kids swam out and joined her.

"Here we are Ben."

The judge called out "On your marks, get ready, Go!" Sherry gave Ben a little nudge and he jumped into the water.

"Swim to us Ben. Come on, you can do it. Keep swimming. Come on Ben."

All the kids were shouting and Penny was jumping up and down waving frantically. The other swimmers were way ahead of Ben. By the time most of them had finished, Ben was still quietly paddling along, smiling, looking at Penny and the other kids. Twice he stopped and stood up, looking at the crowd on shore. Everyone was cheering. Ben would then look at Penny and begin swimming toward her again. Now he was the only one left in the race. The crowd grew hushed. Everyone was watching Ben. He kept swimming and the kids kept encouraging him. Finally, he touched the finish line. There was a brief moment of total silence, and then the shouting and clapping erupted.

Everyone was shouting, "Yeah Ben. Way to go."

Meanwhile, Ben had quietly turned around and was swimming back to the dock where Sherry stood. This was what they had practiced and this was what he was going to do. Everyone was on their feet encouraging him. Many people, including me, were wiping their eyes. Ben finished the race. It wouldn't have happened without those kids being his friends.

Beautiful Ben

Those kids taught Bob and I a huge lesson that summer. We had to let Ben take risks, but we also had to let his friends support him. It didn't always have to be us, his parents, who were there for him.

• •

For the most part, this is how our summers were spent. The only difference now is that it is our grandchildren who get excited about Carnival. I swim in the lake when ever the weather is agreeable. Ben visits often. He is well known now around the lake. People greet him as the canoe or kayak bye. Summers are our respite from stress and tension. Unfortunately, summers always come to an end.

Chapter 9

A new school year, a new school, a new set of problems

After two years of planning, while Ben was at Jowonio, we enrolled him in Waters Elementary School in our little town. We thought we were prepared, but we would never have predicted what happened next. It was about two weeks before the opening day of school. We still had not been told who Ben's teacher would be so I called the school and asked to speak to Mr. Henry, the elementary school principal and chairperson of the Committee on the Handicapped. Since we had been working closely with him preparing for this day, I was confident he would have this information. He knew that we planned to take Ben to the school prior to the first day, meet his new teacher, visit his classroom, find the library and the cafeteria, and see where his bus would arrive. We wanted to help him be ready and feel confident. We didn't want any unnecessary surprises for him.

The school secretary answered the phone.

"Oh, Mrs. Lehr. Mr. Henry is not here. Can you hold please?"

I waited. It seemed to take a long time, but I figured he was out in the building somewhere and she would have to locate him. Finally, a voice that I didn't recognize picked up.

"Mrs. Lehr. This is Mr. Ambrose. I am the acting elementary school principal now. Mr. Henry has left the district. How can I help you?"

I was so shocked I couldn't speak at first. Mr. Henry was gone? Surely this was some mistake. Maybe he was just on vacation resting up before the school year began. I tried to compose myself.

"I wanted to speak to Mr. Henry about my son Ben." I began. "He is entering Waters School from Jowonio, but I..." Before I could continue, Mr. Ambrose abruptly cut me off.

"You can be quite assured, Mrs. Lehr, I am fully aware of who you are and I know everything about your son, Ben." I didn't like his tone, cold and mean, but what came next was even more disturbing.

"Mr. Henry was the person who was in charge of making the decisions regarding Ben's placement. However, now that he has left the district, we will have to reconsider what is most appropriate for Ben. We will be scheduling a new

Beautiful Ben

Committee on the Handicapped meeting within the next several weeks to rewrite Ben's IEP. "

My mind was racing. For two years we had planned that Ben would enter a regular kindergarten class. The teacher would be given training by the staff at Jowonio and he/she would also have the services of a classroom aide to support Ben. He would also receive speech therapy, but would attend regular physical education and all the other special subjects (art, music, library) with his classmates. This had all been agreed to at the COH meeting last spring. Mr. Henry had helped us plan for this. Now, this man who I didn't even know was telling me that they would have to start all over again. How could that be? Suddenly, images of the ED classroom at BOCES loomed in my mind.

My mind was racing. I thought, "Oh, God. Please this can't be happening!" I took a breath, and spoke. I didn't even recognize my voice; it was flat, lifeless, cold.

"Mr. Ambrose, with all due respect, the COH agreed to Ben's IEP last spring. Mr. Henry approved that as the building administrator and the COH chair. Even Mr. Russell, the superintendent approved of this."

Before I could proceed, Mr. Ambrose again interrupted.

"Mr. Russell has also left the district. Any decisions made regarding your son must be reviewed by the new acting superintendent and myself. We cannot proceed until this has occurred. At that point I will convene a new COH meeting and we will invite you to attend."

"Invite me to attend? You have to be joking!" I thought. Suddenly I had a chilling thought, but Mr. Ambrose was continuing to speak.

"In the meantime, Mrs. Lehr, we want you to keep Ben home. We do not have a classroom for him to attend. Nor do we have any teacher who is willing to have someone like him in her classroom."

I felt myself begin to shake.

"What do you mean, keep him home? He has to attend school. I can't keep him home. He expects to go to school just like his sisters."

I didn't know what to say to his "someone like him" comment.

"Well Mrs. Lehr, that is my decision. Keep him home for at least two weeks or until we can figure out what to do. We want to explore the BOCES self-contained classroom for emotionally disturbed children. That might be the most appropriate placement for him." Before I could say anything, Mr. Ambrose thanked me for calling and said he would get back in touch with me when he had more information. He hung up.

I stood there a long time holding the phone before I finally hung up. I was shaking and the tears were slowly running down my cheeks and dripping off my chin. My thoughts were all over the place. Where did Mr. Henry go? Why hadn't he told me he was leaving? What about Mr. Russell? He had been a good ally for us? Where did he go? Why? What about Ben? What should we do? I called Bob at work and thus began our two-year battle with our school district to get Ben an education.

We did send Ben to school that first day. We called the school and said he would be on the bus. We instructed Sherry and Penny to stay with him when they got to school until a teacher arrived. I called Mr. Ambrose and told him Ben would be attending the first day. Mr. Ambrose knew that the previous spring we had visited the kindergarten and first grade classrooms and had agreed that Mrs. Christopher's first grade room would be the best place for Ben. Mr. Henry had concurred. She was organized, energetic, and made learning fun. It was our understanding that Mr. Henry had arranged for Mrs. Christopher's classroom to have only have 15 students along with a classroom aide assigned to support Ben. We wanted Ben to be in Mrs. Christopher's room. Later, we agreed to continue to meet with Mr. Ambrose or whom ever the district identified, but Ben was going to be in Mrs. Christopher's room.

It was his right under the law. Despite the law, it was one of the hardest things we ever did, putting him on the bus that morning. What would happen when he arrived at the school? We firmly believed that Ben deserved to go to school, but were we sacrificing our child for the sake of a principle? We waited for the school to call us, demanding we take him home. The call never came. Ben came home on the bus with Sherry and Penny. They told us that a teacher had met Ben at the bus and taken him with her. Later we learned that this was the special education teacher for the self-contained classroom. She had met the bus and taken Ben to Mrs. Christopher's classroom. She told us that she would be planning for him now, taking him back to her classroom where she would be teaching him daily living skills. I wanted to scream. He didn't need to learn how to brush his teeth and wash his hands. He knew how to do that. We wanted him to get the same academic curriculum as the other children.

For the next several weeks, Ben went to Mrs. Christopher's class for the opening exercises. Then he was escorted to Miss Wilson's class room, where all the other "handicapped' children were sent. It was not what we wanted for Ben, but we felt we had to try to work with the staff. We were afraid for Ben if we created too much animosity.

Beautiful Ben

As the year progressed, things for Ben deteriorated. He was unable to comply with the routines and schedules Mrs. Christopher expected of her first graders. His behavior deteriorated. His communication was limited at best, and this proved frustrating for everyone. Even though he had an aide assigned to him, she had never been with a child with autism before and was not afforded any training. She meant well; she tried hard. What she lacked, however, was the notion that Ben was a complicated child who needed support, support like he had received at Jowonio. The Jowonio teachers had offered to visit, provide training about how to help a child like Ben, and they had offered to give on-going support as needed, but the acting principal refused any of this.

Things got worse. Ben's teacher no longer wanted him in her classroom. Mrs. Christopher had tried in the beginning, but from our perspective, she had never been given the kind of support she should have had. She had parents of her other children complain that she spent too much time with Ben, that he was disruptive and undisciplined. She stopped communicating with us through the little notebook that traveled back and forth in Ben's backpack. For a while the aide would write notes about what Ben did. Usually these began with "It was a really bad day today…" and would then detail what had happened. It didn't take long before Miss Wilson, the special education teacher, began to write the notes and we recognized that Ben was spending more and more time in her classroom. She was a good special education teacher, but this wasn't what we wanted for Ben. We requested meetings but these were often postponed or cancelled. Finally, Mr. Ambrose called to invite us to a COH meeting. We were unprepared for what was to transpire.

After waiting in the hall outside the elementary school conference room where we could see the teachers talking and nodding their heads in agreement, the secretary indicated they were ready for us. We entered the conference room. Mr. Ambrose, Mrs. Christopher, Miss Wilson, and at least 7-8 others were sitting around the table. No one looked up at us. They each had piles of papers and notes in front of them. We felt very intimidated and vulnerable. We sat down and Mr. Ambrose began the meeting.

In a cold and measured voice, never looking directly at either of us, Mr. Ambrose detailed how teachers in the school (he didn't say who) had circulated a petition identifying Ben "as an animal" who could not benefit from schooling. The petition demanded that the school remove him immediately.

"Most of the teachers signed this petition."

He held it up for us to see, but didn't give it to us. We could see a long line of signatures. We were speechless. It didn't make any difference. Mr. Ambrose continued by saying that he had contacted the BOCES administrator and was preparing to have Ben bussed there beginning the next week. We were devastated. Our son? An animal? How could they say this?

Before we could even ask the question, however, Mrs. Christopher shook her hand at us and said angrily,

"He urinated on the playground, right in front of the other children!"

She was outraged. We were dumbfounded and speechless. It didn't make any difference, however, because we were not given any opportunity to speak. Mr. Ambrose was still holding up the petition. How were we to respond to this horrendous accusation? Ben was only a child, six years old. Weren't they, as adults – as teachers - supposed to be teaching him, guiding him, supporting him? No, they were attacking him and us. We just wanted them to see Ben as a child who needed an education. They just wanted us to get him out of their sight and out of their school. He was just a little boy, but they had decided he was "an animal" – their words. They were ganging up on us just like bullies, but we didn't want to give up. We tried to say these things but it was hopeless. The meeting ended quickly. We left shaken and deeply hurt.

That night, Bob and I talked about what had happened. Finally, our anger began to subside and slowly, our conversation turned to the topic of what we could do for Ben.

"What does the law say? What are our rights? Should we keep him there? Where else could he go? What should we do? What should we do?

We knew the law (P.L. 94-142) protected children like Ben, and his rights. We also knew that the law afforded us as his parents, certain rights.

"We need to know how to use the law to help us." Bob was so clear headed. My emotions were about to tip over the edge, but I listened, calmed by his rationality. What do we know about the law and how can we use this for Ben's benefit?" What a great set of questions. We got copies of the law and read it. We didn't know what the school district knew, but we became knowledgeable about what we had a right to ask for. Since it seemed we weren't going to get what we had originally expected, Ben attending the first grade with his non-disabled peers, a smaller classroom, support for his teacher, an instructional aide, and training, we decided to negotiate. I guess we really decided to fight, but it sounded better to say we wanted to negotiate.

We informed Mr. Ambrose that we not only did not agree with his/their recommendation for Ben to be placed at BOCES, we intended to file a "due process" case against them, alleging that they had violated his right to a free and appropriate education. We carefully worded this in a letter sent to the Board of Education.

Our mistake, however, was that we didn't have a lawyer. The school district ignored us. They didn't even respond to our letter. Life was miserable for Bob and I, but we tried to keep life "normal" for the Sherry, Penny and Ben.

We kept waiting for the something to happen; for the school to do something. We heard nothing. We sent Ben off each morning. His bus driver kept us informed, but she didn't want to jeopardize her job so she was careful. She genuinely cared about Ben, but was also scared that she might get fired if she "sided" with us. She was our only source of real information. We were deeply appreciative of her concern for Ben, but we also knew that we were heading into danger.

We tried to maintain a normal family life, what ever that was. I was working full time as the Coordinator of a program for adults with developmental disabilities at a local community college. I had to be on campus four nights a week until around 9:30 PM. Bob was teaching Psychology at SUNY Cortland and would get home to take care of homework, supper, baths, and bedtime while I was at work. The schedules, the pressure, the stress was weighing heavily on Bob and I, but we agreed that we would not make our children's lives suffer. We vowed that we would not talk about what was happening for Ben in front of our children. Even though we felt increasing animosity toward the teachers and district officials, we tried to remain upbeat and positive about school for their sake.

••

A story – Our house should be a fun place for kids

We decided that we would make our house a fun place for other kids to be. We felt that if they wanted to be here, they would get to know Ben and become his friends and allies. We built a really cool playhouse in our back yard, and we made sure that kids on the street knew they were welcome to come and play anytime. We assured the parents that we would be there to supervise. As much as we could, we tried to make sure that Ben was included in what ever the other kids were doing.

"Hi, Mrs. Lehr. I am having a birthday party on Saturday and I wanted to invite Sherry, Penny and Ben to come. Can they?" Jennnifer, our neighbor was speaking. She was just a year older than Sherry and they all had played together on the street. Her sister, Melissa, attended special education classes at the high school. It was the first time Ben had ever been invited to a birthday party.

I almost cried. "Yes, I think they would love to come. What time?"

These little milestones are so important – birthday parties, sleepovers, play dates. Kids like Ben, those with special needs, hardly ever get invited. Why is that? Ben went to Jennnifer's party and had fun. Years later, Jennnifer became Ben's baby sitter. Many years after that, Jennnifer had her own child with special needs, Joshua. She is a wonderful parent. We think some of that had to do with Ben, and of course, with her sister.

· ·

Somehow we made it through that first year and thankfully arrived again at summer. We relaxed and played. Ben went to the Main Dock and had fun with the kids there. Most of them didn't go to the same school as Ben, but they accepted him as part of Main Dock crowd. Many of the people remembered Ben from previous summers and wanted to know how he was doing. They genuinely cared about his welfare. He was part of this community and there was a sense of protection and care that continues even today.

Beautiful Ben

Chapter 10

Yes, it can get worse, and it does

Summer passed quickly, too quickly, and suddenly we were thrown back into the preparations for the fall. The petition was not mentioned again, nor was there any further discussion with us about a transfer to BOCES. The end of the year recommendation had been that Ben should continue in Mrs. Christopher's room and a new classroom aide would be hired. Shortly before school was to start in the fall, Mrs. Camp called to introduce herself as the new classroom aide. She was a parent of another child in the district. She wanted to come to our house to meet Ben. We were encouraged. She tried to interact with Ben but he was too engrossed with swimming and playing – not terribly surprising to us. She was nice and we were hopeful that this year would be better. How wrong we were. Daily we received messages from the teacher about how "it was a terrible day", "it was the worst day ever", "you can't imagine what he did" and so on. Then one day, it all came to a head. We were told that Mrs. Camp was at her wit's end. She was ready to quit. Then, not much later, something else happened that made us realize we had to do something, now.

"Mrs. Lehr, how come they put Ben in the Janitor's closet?" Jimmy asked. It was a simple question asked by a child from our street, but it was shocking.

"What do you mean, Jimmy?" I tried to keep my voice even.

"I saw Mr. Burton, you know - the Janitor, take Ben into his room and lock the door." I stood still, the horror spilling over me like a waterfall.

"Well, Jimmy, that is great question and you better be sure I am going to find out the answer!"

I called the school the next day. I was told that because Ben's behavior was so disruptive to the teachers this was the only thing they could do. So they didn't deny it. They did shut him in the janitor's office!

"How can you do this to a child, my son?" I wanted to scream this into the phone.

"What does Ben do that is so disruptive?" I asked trying to keep my voice calm.

"Well, he really cries a lot. He upsets everyone. We really have no other place to take him. Mr. Burton's broom closet is away from the rest of the classrooms, and it is quiet."

I couldn't believe what I was hearing. A broom closet? I was seething. I think I did scream this time. I am not sure.

"If any other child in the school cried, is this how you would treat him?" As soon as I said this I knew they didn't see Ben as a child – he was a monster, an aberration, an animal who should not be in their presence. I slammed the phone down. This had to stop. We called the local legal aide society.

I want to be fair. I think Mrs. Christopher, Miss Wilson, the classroom aides wanted to do the right thing, but I think the school administration woefully failed them. I think they were good people, good teachers, caring individuals, but they didn't see Ben as a child like the others. They also didn't know how to teach him. Did they ask for help? No one was speaking to us by then, so we didn't know what was going on.

In retrospect, it became clear to us that the administrators set up the staff to be the bad guys. They fed their fears, nurtured their fragile feelings of being inadequate teachers when confronted with someone as complicated as Ben, and never, never, gave them the support and training that would have made the difference. Over the years I have felt such pain and animosity toward these people. I just don't understand how you can call yourself an educator, but then decide which children are worthy of teaching. Of course, I realize now how the teachers believed they didn't need to know how to teach "special children" – that was what special educators did. I didn't understand why regular and special education teachers seemed so unwilling to learn and change. Each seemed to protect their respective disciplines. Everyone, but me, seemed comfortable with this arrangement. In my mind, separate was not equal. Besides, when I had begun my teaching career in 1964, I had special education students in my Physical Education and General Health classes. I was expected to learn how to reach them. I was never given the option to "get rid" of them. The administration and other teachers, especially the special education staff, helped me. That was all I wanted for Ben. It took me a long time to understand the impact of professionalism and specialization in such fields as education. Of course, I realize now how these regular education teachers believed they didn't need to know how to teach special education students. It wasn't their job to know. That was what Special Education teachers were for. I simply was not able to recognize this professional distinction.

One other thing I learned in my professional career as a teacher educator and consultant, teachers are at the mercy of their building administrators. Had I known this when Ben was there, I might have acted differently. I might have tried to be more understanding and cooperative. But I didn't know this, and I did believe that teachers were supposed to educate children to the best of their ability.

It was time to go to court

We knew the law. We had learned this in self-defense. Syracuse University and the Center on Human Policy had helped us to learn about our rights as parents. We knew the school district was violating the law. We knew Ben was being hurt, but the decision to go to court was so scary. Once we headed down this path, there was no turning back. We were frightened of what this might mean for Sherry and Penny. They were still in the school system. We worried feverishly about the costs involved financially. Could we afford to do this? Who would be there to help us? Were we doing the right thing? All we wanted was for Ben to be in the same classroom as his peers, receiving the same educational curriculum, the same chance to be productive and happy. Why was this so much to ask? Were we doing the right thing? Should we accept that he would never amount to anything; that he would end up living in a group home and working in a sheltered workshop? We knew the answer to these last questions. We knew, without a doubt, that we weren't going to give up on Ben now, and we weren't going to let his opportunities be limited because he had autism. He was only a child. We could not write him off that soon, that quickly. We had to fight!

"Well, this is not going to be easy." A young female attorney was speaking softly to us. She sat with three other women – all attorneys. They had agreed to hear our case – to see if they could represent us. Fighting a school district is never easy.

She continued. "But you just might have a case here. We need some time to review the documents." We agreed to meet again within a week. For the first time Bob and I felt we were not alone. We knew the folks at Jowonio supported our efforts to have Ben included, but having attorneys agree gave us added hope. We waited.

Horn, Heins, Finkelstein and Pezzulo – a real law firm, was going to represent us. After preliminary discussions of the nature of our case and what might be involved for them, they set a cap on their fees. Later, we would all laugh about what a great idea this was, although the cap should have been so much higher. They filed an official "due process" hearing request on our behalf. As they say in the military – the battle lines were drawn.

In the meantime, Bob and I tried desperately to maintain a normal family life, what ever that was. We tried not to talk about the lawsuit in front of the children. We tried to remain positive and tell them that they were getting a wonderful education, even though we felt so conflicted. One day, however, Sherry confronted us.

"What is going on? I don't understand. Why are the teachers so angry with you and Dad?" She queried.

I could see the strain in her face and hear the frustration in her voice, but I was unwilling to admit she had figured out that something was wrong. We had tried so desperately to protect her and Penny.

"What do you mean?" I asked, trying to sound innocent.

"Come on Mom, you know what I mean. What is happening with Ben? What is going on? Today, one of my teachers asked me 'Do you know how much your parents are costing this school district?' Mom, what was I supposed to say? I don't know what's going on. He is my brother. You have to tell me what is happening."

She was right, of course, but I was reluctant to let down my guard. I wanted to protect her, and Penny and Ben. This accusation from her teacher, however, forced me to realize that ignorant protection was not what anyone needed.

"Well, honey, it is a tough story, and Ben is the victim, but so are you and Penny. Daddy and I are fighting with the school district so that Ben can have the same rights as you two – to get a good education. They want to send him to a BOCES classroom for emotionally disturbed children and Daddy and I don't want that. We are fighting to keep Ben in school. The teachers are angry because they think we are wrong. We have tried to protect you both so that you won't get caught up in this mess. I am sorry your teacher said that to you today." I could see from her face that Sherry was furious.

"What do you mean, you want to protect us?" It was an accusation, not a question.

"Ben is my brother. He is my brother!" she shouted at me.

"Oh my God," I thought. "Now even my kids are against me. I just want to do what is right."

Court Proceedings

A court date was set and the due process proceedings should have begun. We were informed that the school district had hired a law firm experienced in educational law to represent them. Mr. Harris was their lead attorney and the man with whom we and our law firm were to arrange meeting times. A due process hearing officer had been appointed. Nothing happened. Each time a hearing date was set, Mr. Harris would cancel. These hearing appointments were usually scheduled at his office, a 45-minute drive for us. We would arrange our work schedules so that we could to be there, and we arranged after school care when necessary. We would arrive with our attorneys only to be shown into a waiting room where we would do just that, wait.

"Mr. Harris had an illness in the family. He will be late, but he will be here." His secretary told us. We waited, one, two hours. No one showed. Finally, we were invited to reschedule. What choice did we have? On another occasion, we were told that Mr. Harris had been detained by another case. We were assured that he would be arriving shortly. We just had to be patient and wait. Of course, after one, two hours, we were invited to reschedule.

Ms. Heins, our lead attorney, was perseverant, even relentless. She would reschedule and prep witnesses. She and her colleagues helped us understand the stalling strategy used by Mr. Harris and the other attorneys. We assured her that, no matter what, we were not going to give up. We fundamentally believed that Ben had a right to a free and appropriate education and we were going to do everything within our power to see that he got it.

The hearing dragged on and on, month after month. Our nerves were frayed and our emotions were totally raw. Some days we would actually be able to present testimony and hear witnesses. Some days we just waited. It was gruesome. What sustained us was the support of our friends from Jowonio and our attorneys. They coached us about what to expect and how to think about the questions we were being asked. One lesson we learned from Ms. Heins was that a good attorney should never ask a question that he/she cannot anticipate the answer to.

"Watch for these," she said. "When they come give the best answer you can to get important information on the record." It was an important lesson, one we kept in mind when each question was posed.

As the hearing continued, Bob and I were also working with other parents who were trying to establish a new program within the Syracuse City School District, a continuation of the Jowonio program for children who were aging out. The goal of the program was to enable these children to transition into the city school system and continue within an integrated school environment. Professors from Syracuse University's Special Education Department offered to work with the city school staff to make this work. The departmental chair and the Dean of Education were on board with this and their support appealed to the Superintendent.

Crying for help, but we didn't understand

Meanwhile, for Ben, things were deteriorating. He was becoming increasingly unhappy. He was engaging in some self-abuse at home, hitting himself, pinching his arms and face, slapping his neck, pinching his sides. He rarely slept more than a few hours at a time. He would cry when it was time to go to school. He began to destroy things in our house. It started with electric cords. Ben would use scissors or knives from our kitchen drawers to cut though electric cords. He would short out the cords; sparks would fly and the appliance or lamp was destroyed. We gathered the implements that Ben might use and locked them in cabinets. It made living a normal life difficult, but we felt we needed to help Ben and if this worked, we would do it. We didn't find all the knives. There were some in Bob's shop or with our camping gear. Ben would search these out and once he found them, he would start cutting his arms and legs – nice tidy little slices. It was gruesome. We tried to prevent this, but we had to sleep sometimes and he would prowl, looking for tools he could use to cut – himself, electric cords, his hair, clothes.

We didn't realize what a cry for help this was. We tried to prevent to protect. One morning I came down the stairs and stopped cold in my tracks. My supper table had been gouged, cut, sliced. This table was an antique solid oak pedestal table, 10 feet long by 4 feet wide. Ben had found a knife or something and methodically cut wedges of wood out of the entire edge – all the way around the table. I was stunned. Slowly I looked at the devastation, but I could not comprehend the feelings that had motivated Ben. Something caught my eye and I looked at the moulding around the doors into the dining room. Each of them had been systematically gouged; everything had been cut, destroyed. I knew I was crying, but there was no sound out of me. I just stood in abject horror wondering what to do. I still didn't get the enormity of the pain that Ben must have been feeling to do this. All I could think about was how to make this better.

He was sleeping. I found him tucked quietly in his bed, peaceful. I wanted to scream, hit him, make him feel as miserable as I did, but I couldn't. I looked at him and realized I had to be the one in control. I let him sleep. Later when he awoke and had some breakfast, I told him that I expected him to sand each gouge and repair them as best he could. I gave him some sand paper and helped him get started. He didn't resist.

"Why did you do this?" I asked. He didn't answer. He just looked at me.

Another time, it was Thanksgiving vacation; I awoke early and came down stairs to make the morning coffee. We had been remodeling our house and had spent the past several days carefully putting pink fiberglass insulation in the ceiling of the

Beautiful Ben

family room. It had been a messy job, but we had done it. Now all we needed was the plastic backing and the sheet rock. As I walked into the kitchen, which opens into the family room, my mouth dropped. All the insulation from the ceiling had been removed and was piled neatly in a huge pink pile in the middle of the family room. "Ben." I exhaled his name quietly through my teeth. I felt defeated. Later, Bob and I carefully discarded the insulation in plastic garbage bags. We never said anything to Ben. We just didn't think he could understand. What we were missing, of course, was that Ben was trying to tell us that he was terribly upset; something was wrong. I guess he thought that by upsetting us, we would realize that he was upset. Unfortunately, we just didn't understand this way of communicating. We didn't get it. How very sad. I still feel guilty that I didn't recognize that Ben had feelings. He was sensitive to what was going on, too.

We didn't punish him. What good would it do? We did tell him in no uncertain terms that what he had done was wrong. We realized much later that he knew that. We just didn't get that he was so upset and was trying to implore us for help.

A resolution is in sight

Even though we tried desperately to protect Ben and our daughters from the strain that the hearing was causing us, it was becoming increasingly evident that we were failing. We tried not to talk about the hearing, but phone calls would have to be answered, and papers compiled. Everyone was beginning to suffer. Bob and I were sure we were doing the right thing for Ben, but we began to question if Sherry and Penny were going to survive unscathed. Would we make it?

After a particularly long delay in scheduling the next hearing meeting, our attorneys explained that it was likely that this stalling tactic could go on forever. The district was probably hoping to wear us down and wear us out. We agreed that they were beginning to succeed, but with the support of our attorneys and friends, we explored our options and arrived as some new strategies. According to the attorney for the school district, we had two options. One, we could accept the district's recommendations that Ben either go into a self-contained program for children with emotional disturbances at the local BOCES center, or he could be assigned to a self contained "for special education students only" program in the school he was now attending. They also suggested that we might want to explore a residential center for "children like Ben" and, if we agreed, they would consider paying the tuition. Of course, we rejected all of these. The residential center was definitely out of the question. We talked a lot about the other two options. What would Ben's future look like if we chose either of these? Eventually, either way, he would end up in a BOCES program for

Emotionally Disturbed kids. After graduation he would predictably be transferred to the local sheltered employment center or possibly some residential institution.

The school year was rapidly coming to an end. Anxiously, we looked forward to the relief of the summer; we were so overwhelmed by the stress. By this point, Bob and I knew were barely holding it together. We knew we would never give up, but the constancy of the tension and the insidious pressure were almost unbearable. There had to be something we could do. There was.

After lengthy discussions with our attorneys we agreed on a new strategy. We made a counter proposal. We knew that the "stay put" option within the PL 94-142 law mandated that the student must be kept in his/her current placement until the hearing determination had been made. However, we all agreed that this would be a disaster for Ben. The school didn't want him to "stay put" any longer in their elementary building, and we didn't want him to go into a segregated, for "handicapped students only" site.

Ms. Heins and our other attorneys offered the idea that, as an interim solution the hearing officer could temporarily place Ben in the newly developing Integrated Autistic Program in the Syracuse City School District until the results of the hearing had been determined. The Waters School District administrator readily agreed. The Syracuse District also agreed. They needed to fill the grade level classrooms and since our district agreed to pay the state reimbursement rate for tuition plus transportation, it seemed like a win-win for everyone. We were deeply saddened to think that Ben would not be able to go to school with his neighborhood peers. Life was going to change for all of us. Would it be better? I guess we finally realized that it couldn't get any worse; or so we thought.

Did we feel defeated? Yes and no. Yes, because we had to finally give up on our dream that Ben would be in a local classroom of his neighborhood peers and that his teachers would care about him as a person; a legitimate member of their class and school. No, because we were able to hold on to our belief that Ben had a fundamental and legal right to a free and appropriate education as described in the public law. It just wasn't going to happen in our local district. We also didn't feel defeated because we were able to include in our testimony in the hearing that Ben could have been successful in our local school, if he and the teachers had received sufficient support and training. That this support never happened was a clear statement of the failure of the local district to be responsible. That was important to us, to know that they had failed their own teaches and ultimately Ben, our daughters, and us. School ended and so did the hearing. Summer began and we all took a deep sigh – we needed the rest. September was a long way off, thank god. What would it bring? I just couldn't think about it yet.

Chapter 11

My life changes - a new career opens

During the hearing and while Ben, Sherry and Penny were going to school each day, Bob and I continued to work. Bob was a college professor. I worked in a variety of different jobs all related to the disability field. My first "real job" after completing my master's degree in Health Education was as a program coordinator for "College for Living." This was a continuing education program based at the local community college that offered recreational and remedial courses for individuals with developmental disabilities over the age of 18. The program had been open for about year when I was hired. The first coordinator was unhappy with the administrative duties and wanted to return to being a recreational therapist. I had seen the ad in the Sunday Employment section of the newspaper and had sent in my resume and cover letter, never expecting to hear anything back. I had been applying for other jobs, but this one seemed really exciting.

I didn't want to get my hopes up, but when I was invited for an interview my heart raced. I can do this job well, I would think, in my most optimistic moments, and then my doubts would crowd my brain – "what do you know about administration of programs? What do you know about people with developmental disabilities? What do you know about community college policies and inclusion of adults with disabilities at the adult level?"

As Bob would say, "You don't know squat." He didn't mean to put me down. He was right. I had experience with one child, my son with autism, but I also had the knowledge I had gained from Jowonio and I figured I had nothing to lose by going through the interview. However, I have always had problems with feeling insecure, or inadequate. All of my fears of failure slam me in the face. Today, my friends would laugh if they heard me say how insecure I was then. Living with and loving Bob had given me confidence in myself, but I really wanted to try.

It was summer and very hot. I went to an old house on the edge of Syracuse University campus for the interview. The building was the home of the Center on Human Policy, an advocacy center based at the university for people with disabilities. I waited nervously in the reception area chatting with Helen, the secretary. She grilled me, a bit of a curmudgeon I thought, but I liked her. She was blunt and honest.

It was my turn. The candidate before me, a man dressed in a snappy suit and tie smiled knowingly as he left the building. Helen showed me into the interview room and I was totally shocked. There was a huge conference table around which were seated at least 12 people. I am not sure what I expected, but this certainly wasn't it. There was an open seat and I sat. I wasn't sure who was in charge or how the interview would proceed. I searched the faces around the table and came upon Ellen Barnes from Jowonio. She smiled, and I relaxed. "Be yourself," I said to myself, "and say what you believe."

I have no idea how long the interview went or what was said, but I knew I felt good about what had happened. Even if I didn't get the job I knew that I had found the work I wanted to do. The next morning I received a call saying that I was being offered the job. I would be working for the state on a civil service line, which meant a salary and benefits. I would be based at the community college, but I would be supervised by the people who had interviewed me.

"Would I accept?" She asked. I knew I should say that I had to consider the salary and all that stuff, but I was too excited.

"Of course I want the job." I heard myself saying.

Our new life begins

So, as Ben prepared to begin his new life in the Syracuse City School District in third grade, I began a new professional life as the Program Coordinator of the College for Living at Onondaga Community College in Syracuse. Also, after a lot of thought, Bob and I withdrew Sherry and Penny from Waters and enrolled them in a private school in Syracuse. This decision really strapped us financially, but it was the right thing for us.

Only Bob seemed stable. We knew our lives would fundamentally change. We hoped for the better. The logistics, however, were a bit daunting. Our local school readily agreed to bus Ben to his new school, but they refused to allow Sherry and Penny to travel with him to their new school even though they were only a few miles apart.

The Waters "little yellow bus" would wait at the bus stop at the end of our one-mile long dead end road each morning by 7:15AM. The school bus would not pick him up at our house because it was a private road; at least that is what we were told. So Sherry, Penny, Ben and I would go to the bus stop at the end of our road where Ben would get on the bus. Then I would drive Sherry and Penny to their school, no more than a few miles away from Ben's school. Often we followed Ben's bus on the interstate, turning off just one exit before he did.

"Oh no, Mrs. Lehr" the director of transportation for our home school district was speaking, "we can't transport your daughters. They aren't classified as special education students."

We were just too tired to challenge this ruling so I drove them to school each day. Their school was on the east side of the city and then I would drive across town to the west side, where my office was located at the community college. In the afternoon, I would reverse the trip, hurrying to get home in time to meet Ben at the bus stop. Once the girls became involved in sports and after school activities, Bob and I would negotiate who would be there to meet Ben's bus, and who would get the girls and drive them home. Often I had to work late into the afternoon or evenings which meant Bob had to meet Ben's bus, get to Syracuse to get the girls and be there helping with homework, dinner, baths and bedtime until I could get home. It was stressful and required great skill at scheduling and patience, but we felt it was better than what we had gone through for the past few years. Besides, Penny, Sherry and I enjoyed the commuting time talking and laughing together. It wasn't so bad.

The two years we spent battling with Waters School District had been arduous. Certainly, it had cost lots of money, but it had cost even more in terms of our trust of professionals. We now were guarded; protective, scared that Ben would be isolated and hurt again. We were guardedly optimistic that his experiences in Syracuse would be better. We also knew we would be more vigilant and careful but we were unsure how to accomplish this since Ben would no longer be in the same school as his neighbors and his sisters. It was going to be entirely new, and we were truly apprehensive. We also felt alone now. The support of our friends at Jowonio was still there, but it would be different now that Ben was not in that school. Our neighbors were not interested in what happened to Ben or us. We were new in the community, and although the kids had accepted us, it was harder for the adults, especially those affiliated with the school district. Ben was the first black student at the school and the first child with autism. I guess we should have expected people to be confused or wary, and we sort of did. But what hurt so badly was that Ben was just a small child. He didn't choose to have autism. He wasn't trying to make people upset. Why couldn't people see this? Why did they have to hurt him, not help him? I still ask these fundamental questions.

Graduate School

It didn't take me long in my new job to connect with the faculty in the School of Education at Syracuse University. They were approachable and eager to help my students and me. I had never considered going back to school after I had finished my master's degree in Health Education, but several of the professors said I should consider applying to one of their doctoral programs. Although I was flattered, I simply didn't think I was smart enough to persue this kind of a degree.

Bob was quick to respond. "Of course you are. You just need to build more confidence in yourself. Take your time." Little did either of us realize, at the time, that it would eventually take me almost thirteen years to complete my Ph.D. in Special Education. In the beginning, before I was accepted, I thought I wanted to become a special education administrator so that il could change to system that had impeded Ben's access into the regular classroom. I interviewed special education administrators seeking their advice about what had motivated them to follow this career path. I wasn't particularly comfortable with their answers nor with the suggestions some administrators made about how to get a good job. I still naively wanted to change the world; getting the job was simply the pathway.

One motivation that I had for enrolling in graduate school was to help other parents like us who were fighting to get their son or daughter into a regular class or activity. I would go to meetings about their child or his or her school program, but was regularly discounted as "just a parent" or "only a mom" or "someone who can't understand" referring to the classroom or the bureaucracy that had to be negotiated in schools. Like many of the parents I had come to know, I was patronized and dismissed. It infuriated me as much as it did sadden me. Once in a meeting I was asked to identify by credentials before I would be permitted to speak. I sat up straight and said I have a M.O.M degree. When they laughed, I vowed silently to get my Ph.D. degree too.

After almost five years as the administrator of the College for Living program, I accepted a job at the Center on Human Poliicy at Syracuse University. I was tired of working four nights a week, and this new job would cover my graduate tuition. My work was as a consultant to the Technical Assistance to Parent Programs (TAPP), a federally funded program administered by the Federation for Children with Special Needs in Boston, MA. Their mandate was to establish Parent Training and Infomration (PTIs) Centers in every state where parents of children with disabilities could receive information, support, and training regarding the implementation of P.L.94-142 – the Education for All Handicapped Childrens' Act, later reauthorized as the Individuals with Disabilities Education Act (IDEA). My primary responsibility was to write materials in "parent friendly terminology" that explained different provisions of the law, such as transition, health care issues, and the least restrictive environment or inclusion as it was later called.. In addition, I was to work closely with the Federation to organize and host an annual conference for PTI staff, teachers and school administrators, and federal officials in Washington, DC. Through the five years I worked on this project I met many different families and professionals, as well as people with disabilities. It was one of the most exciting learning experiences of my life. The families and people with disabiliites of all ages taught me so much about the bureacracies they had to negotiate, and about thier own resilience, compassion, humor, and love.

When the funding for this project ended, I was offered a research position with the Facilitated Communication Institute which had just been established by Doug Biklen at Syracuse University. I continued taking my graduate courses each of which enriched my thinking. I learned about the rigors of qualitative research and loved it. I began to think of different disseration topics. At first, I wanted to write a biography of Gunnar Dybwad, a truly remarkable man who had influenced the field of national and international disabilities with his commitment to the closure of institutions and to improving the lives of people with mental retardation. I was fortunatel to be able to spend so much time with Gunnar and his wife Rosemary so that I could interview them and learn from them. Finally, I wrote a few draft chapters and showed them to Gunnar. He was deeply hurt and offended by my style of showing him as a common man with uncommon zeal and dedication. He didn't want to be seen in this way. He wanted to be remembered as an historic authority; of course he was, but my writing about his humanity made him feel I had diminshed him. I put away my work on Gunnar.

My new research topic took me into the homes of ten families whose son or daughter had been successfully using facilitated communication. I wanted to know how this affected their relationship and the ways in which the parents perceived their child. I had heard more than one parent describe their child as if they were giving birth all over again, but now to a new person who could communicate in ways that the parents had never thought possible. By this time, Ben was facilitating so I could apprecieate the depth of their feelings. I spent about a year being with these families, listening to them and participating in their family gatherings, trying to make sense of what they were experiencing. Their insights were powerful, but what impacted me the most was the perseverence and resilience with which these families sustained themselves. I was humbled by them.

Although I think many of my professors and even my family were unsure if I would ever finish, I did. It was hard to finish becuase I loved being in school (this was the first time I had this feeling) and I loved working with my professors, with the families and with the people with disabilities. I didn't want to lose these connections and this feeling, but one day Bob asked me, "You do intend to finish, don't you?" I knew it was time.

I continued to work at Syracuse University in several different positions, but eventually I knew I had to move on. I accepted a job teaching Early Childhood Education at a local private college, but it was not a good match. I missed the rigors of teaching graduate level courses, and I missed the cultural milieu of a larger institution. Within three years, I had accepted a job at SUNY Cortland, where Bob taught, in their Education Department. I taught regular and special education classes at the undergraduate and graduate levels. I was also involved in the development of their Inclusive Elementary Education major, and subsequently a parallel graduate major. Both were approved by the New York State Education Department, and they each received national accreditation. My final effort, before retiring in 2005, was to establish the Insitute for Disabiity Studies, a research center focused on learning about disaiblities issues from people with disabilities, their families, and societies in all parts of the world.

Chapter 12

Elementary School and Beyond

In the fall of 1982 Ben entered the Syracuse City School District Integrated Autistic Program at the third grade level. He had been assigned to a class room that would be team taught by Karen Hubby, a certified elementary teacher, and Patricia Floyd, a certified special education and elementary education teacher. Although they were introduced to Ben as Ms. Hubby and Ms. Floyd, he quickly adopted the universal name of "Flubby" for both of them. Rather than being offended, they thought it was funny. Bob and I sighed with relief. Maybe, just maybe, Ben would get a real education.

Ms. Floyd, as the special education teacher, would have primary responsibility for Ben, his program, and his survival. We met with her early on and it was evident that our battle scars from the previous two years showed; we were still raw and guarded. We had no idea what she had been told, but we could tell she was wary of us. Later, she told us we had a reputation as "litigious parents" and she was warned to be careful. What a welcoming for us.

When we first met Ms. Floyd and the rest of the staff, we had so many questions. Would Ben be hurt here, would they treat him like he was an animal, would they expect him to behave just like the other children, would they isolate him, would they…our questions hung in the air like balloons filled with sand.

"My name is Pat Floyd. I will be Ben's teacher. I am a good teacher. That is my job and I will do it well. I am not here to hurt him or do anything other than be his teacher. Now, let's get on with it." Bob and I appreciated that she was straightforward with us, but what would it be like on a daily basis.

It was difficult because Ben was now going to school so far from home. We had no allies or witnesses in the school building to be sure he was safe, but Ben became our informant. He would come home happy. Notebooks filled with information about what his day had included were tucked into his backpack along with papers and evidence of his efforts to achieve academically. Ms. Floyd, Ms. Hubby or some professional would describe some activity that Ben had participated in and asked us to talk with him about this. They told us what concepts they were working on in Math or Reading and asked us to reinforce some of these at home. Finally, someone was asking us to help in Ben's education. It was welcome and refreshing.

Beautiful Ben

Herb Lovett (a friend, advocate for people with disabilities, and scholar) used to say, "It's all about relationships." He was so right. What he meant was, if people get to know someone like Ben, their friendship will allow good things to happen. A friend will help Ben, advocate for him, be there for him. We learned this as part of our efforts to arrange transportation to Ben's new school. For the previous two years Ben had walked with his two sisters and the other kids on the street to and from the bus stop. We always liked this chance for Ben to be part of the community of kids. They became his friends and playmates. Now, however, Ben was being transported on a separate bus. The scheduled times did not match the local bus run for our daughters and other kids. The director of transportation informed us of the pick-up and drop-off schedule, who else would be on the bus, what other stops would be necessary, and who the bus driver would be. Her name was Jane, a diamond in the rough. There were 3-5 other kids on this "special bus" all of whom had some kind of a disability and were being transported to special programs around the county, depending upon their needs. Jane made sure everyone was securely fastened into their seat belts, and she arranged for a special seat for each child. She didn't want to be distracted by kids picking on each other so she tried to keep them separate. That didn't stop Ben from trying to grab or hit other kids, especially one girl about Ben's age. In retrospect, we think Ben was attracted to her, but had no way of saying anything. Jane ruled the bus with an iron hand.

"No monkey business. Keep your hands to yourself. I am in charge here. You will listen to me and behave."

She was clear, stern, yet it became apparent to us that she deeply cared about her "children" and her job.

She would greet Ben each morning with a friendly "Welcome back, Ben." Or "Today is Tuesday. Are you ready to go?"

She would also spare a few minutes to chat with me, especially when she returned Ben in the afternoon. I always appreciated these moments because she would relay information from Ben's teachers, or tell me about something he had done on the bus, or how he would often sing while riding.

Jane remained Ben's driver until he graduated from high school. Eventually, the other students were transported on other buses, mostly to accommodate their schedules. Jane and Ben formed a strong bond, but that didn't stop him from challenging her. For a period of time he tried to grab her arm when she was driving. The director of transportation wanted to put Ben in restraints, but we refused. We asked if he could be seated in the back seat of the bus and have his seat belt fastened in such a way that only Jane could unbuckle it. The director hesitated, but

Sue Lehr

Jane was willing to try this. She knew, and told me later, that she understood that Ben didn't want to hurt her.

"I think the ride just gets to him after a while." She commented.

it took about 45 minutes one way, so she certainly could have been right. This new arrangement seemed to work.

....

A Story – Transportation and the Bus Driver

When Penny transferred to a city high school in her sophomore year, we asked the Waters School District if she could be transported on the same bus since Ben's junior high school building was only about a mile away, and Jane passed right by the high school on to the way to Ben's junior high.

The district transportation officials refused saying that Penny was not a student with a disability and the Committee on Special Education had not approved of transportation for her because of this. A the time, I was working in the city so generally I was able to drive Penny to school, but it often frustrtated me to see Ben and Jane n the bus in front of us on the highway. It also meant that I had to arrange to pick Penny up when school was out and literally fly home in time to meet Ben's bus. We simply made it work and I did love this time with Penny. She is very funny and our rides were often filled with laughter. I needed that.

One particular day, however, I could not drive Penny to school. We had no public transportation in our community so the choice was to let her stay home for the day or approach Jane. Bob was out of town at a conference. That morning, I chatted with Jane a bit, and then explained my problem and asked if Penny could ride the bus that day. She hesitated. She looked at Penny and then sat in her driver's seat for a few minutes. I waited.

"You know, since Ben is the only person on this bus I don't inspect the back seats. Once he is strapped into the front seat next to me, I get on my way. I look in the rear view mirror, of course, but I don't expect to see any other faces, because no one else is there." Then she quietly go out of the driver's seat of the bus and invited me to step away from the bus door.

Let's go chat over there. I want to look at the Iris growing over there, and I want to stretch my legs."

I got her unspoken message. Penny quickly climbed into the bus and scrunched down on the back seat. From outside it was impossible to know there was anyone else on the bus. I wanted to hug Jane, but I knew I could not acknowledge the risk she was taking for us. She knew I would never say anything to the school about this. She trusted me to be discreet and I trusted her to be compassionate. Penny never said a word.

• •

Ben loved Jane. I know Jane grew to care deeply about Ben, too. Sometimes she would bring along cookies or other treats for him. She liked it when he brought his Walkman and would listen to music and sing along. Now, more that 15 years later, we still receive a holiday card and letter from Jane who now lives out of state. We are grateful to Jane for her belief in Ben and her ability to see him as a young person struggling though school just like other kids.

The year flew by; Sherry and Penny were easily acclimating to their new school, each blossoming in their own ways.

The Third Grade Musical

As spring approached, the focus of the third grade turned to their annual musical. This was a production that involved every third grade child, with no exceptions for complicated kids like Ben. Ms. Floyd's task was to figure out the kinds of supports Ben would need to successfully participate in this gala production. Just getting him on the stage would be a challenge, so Ms. Floyd worked with the other students in Ben's class to develop a strategy to make this happen. He was also expected to sing with the whole third grade ensemble. Ben loved to sing, but often would be a few measures behind everyone else. Singing along with his peers and learning the words of all the songs…could he do that? Ms. Floyd was confident that Ben would make it. We weren't so sure. Most important, however, Ben was to remain calm and be a regular participant in the musical when it was performed for the other elementary students (aka a rehearsal) and later in the evening for the families. This was not going to be easy.

"Forty-five minutes on stage? With all the other kids and teachers from the school watching! Administrators and parents too! I can't stand this."

I felt the pressure mounting and was keenly aware that Ben was being caught up in the excitement and the frenzy leading to the performance. I truly had my doubts that he could make it. I wasn't even sure I could make it.

The night of the production, we dropped Ben off at the Music Room and then went to the auditorium to find seats. Bob and I sat nervously anticipating someone asking us to come and get Ben. We were sure he would be too disruptive to "make it" and we were ready for this. I had a headache and I felt slightly nauseous. I was sweating and I felt shaky. I could only imagine how Ben felt. We waited anxiously. As every teacher approached the aisle we were sitting in, I anticipated being called to the music room where the performers were nervously waiting. It didn't happen. The teachers would smile and give us a "thumbs up" sign. My eyes were tearing up, but I was still scared of what might happen.

The first chords of the piano signaled the children to file toward the stage. We craned our necks watching for Ben, when suddenly we saw him marching along; one hand on the shoulder of the student in front of him while the child behind held his other hand. These third grade students made sure Ben got onto the stage, up the bleachers, and to his position. They held his hands, talked to him, rubbed his back. It was hard for Bob and I to see it all; our eyes were teary. Ben was in the chorus and they began to sing. He has always loved music and we could see him visibly relax, but what happened next was more than we could imagine. As the third graders sang, Ben would open and close his mouth just like he was singing. He looked just like the other kids; his mouth opening and closing. If our eyes were misty before, tears were openly flowing down our cheeks now. He was singing, having fun, and performing. He was part of his class. He was just one of the kids and it was – just so very ordinary and extraordinary at the same time. When the show was over, the kids filed off the bleachers, Ben's hands holding those of the kids next to him, and he was smiling. Bob and I were beaming.

This is what it is all about, inclusion, being with your peers, among them. Ben had done it because his teachers and peers expected him to. They had figured out what kind of support he needed because they cared about him and valued his presence. He was one of the third graders at Ed Smith Elementary School, and as such, he had a right and a responsibility to be part of what they all did.

Summer arrived again

The school year ended. We asked Ms. Floyd (we called her Pat now, although Ben still called her "Flubby"), would she consider having Ben spend some time with her each day during the summer "hanging out" where the other kids did. We would take him to meet her each day, and we would pay her for her time. She had formed such a positive relationship with Ben. We also knew that as a teacher she could keep Ben actively involved with the other kids in his class and school at the pool and

Beautiful Ben

playground. We couldn't do that because we didn't live there. She agreed and that was the beginning of a deep friendship between Pat Floyd and myself, and a lasting friendship between "Floyd" and Ben. To this day he calls her "Floyd" and delights in seeing her and her family.

• •

A story – Noah Biklen – It's all in your perspective

I heard this story years later, but I think it is a clear metaphor for how we adults need to model acceptance of disabilities for our children. One of Ben's classmates in the "Flubby" third grade classroom was Noah. His father, Doug Biklen, now Dean of Education at Syracuse University, was my professor, mentor and friend. When this episode happened, however, I had just enrolled in the Ph.D. program in special education at Syracuse University. Doug was my advisor. As Doug would later tell me, one night at the supper table he had said to Noah, now a fourth grader, "so how is Ben Lehr doing?" Noah answered, "Gee Dad, he must be really smart. Did you know he skipped a grade?"

• •

What a positive image of Ben. In reality, Ben had been moved from the "Flubby" third grade classroom to a fifth grade room with Mr. Maruso, not because he was "doing so well or was really smart", but because Mr. Maruso and Mrs. Mathews were willing to have him in their classroom. The fourth grade teachers were not ready yet.

Like the third grade team, the fifth grade team planned together. They seriously considered different positive ways for all kids to access the curriculum and to engage socially. They figured out individual ways for each child like Ben to be supported. Their goal was success for all their kids. They also believed that school should be a fun and interesting place to learn.

Of course, Ben had his behavioral challenges. Most of his problems resulted in him hurting himself, pinching, banging his head on the edge of the doorjamb, or slapping himself. Often he would cry loudly. Rather than punish him for these transgressions, Mr. Marusa understood that Ben was really in distress. He wasn't trying to be belligerent. He was trying to communicate something about how he felt or his confusion about what was going on.

For Ben's entire life, he is now in his mid thirties, he has hurt himself in various ways. It has been one of the most gruesome aspects of his autism. It is so hard to watch him claw at his face, or slap his neck until welts appear, or experience him pinching his arms until they bleed. For a while, as a young child and later, when he was in high school, he would cut himself with sharp knives. With a surgeon's precision he would draw the knife in sharp parallel lines across his forearms or his legs.

Today, psychologists and psychiatrists treat young people for "cutting" themselves. At the time, we all simply saw this as a new and more sophisticated "behavior", a new manifestation of his autism. Of course, we tried to keep knives hidden, and we tried to interrupt his slapping and gouging, but generally we were unsuccessful. We knew he didn't want to hurt us, although invariably that happened. Sometimes he did try to hurt us purposefully, but we didn't understand why. Ben had several explanations.

Sometimes he just wanted to annoy us. Perhaps we would give up and leave him alone. Other times he wanted to make a point.

I WAS WIERD TO HINM SO THAQRT H E COUILDS ASEE QJHAT AUTISM WAS LIKEWE (I was weird to him so that he could see what Autism was like.)

If I really ignored him when this was happening he would grab my arm and look beseechingly into my eyes. Often he would scratch my arm or grab it so hard, I would wince with pain.

Behavior Problems – what is going on?

Ben's oral language was always limited. He often used nonsensical phrases and repeated them to the point that we would shout "shut up!!!!!" He was driving us crazy. One phrase that we all initially laughed at was "Pull the ends". What the hell did that mean? "Pull the ends, pull the ends, pull the ends, pull the ends…" and on it went. "AARGH!!!!!!!!!!!" As Charley Brown would say. We tried to figure out his message. For years we were unsuccessful. It was so frustrating. What we were missing was that we never looked more holistically at what was happening at the time. As a behaviorist, Bob had been trained to search for reinforcement contingencies, but we just couldn't comprehend what Ben was getting from this nonsensical mantra. At one point we thought that his reinforcement was our reactions. He was getting his "jollies" because we were reacting. So we tried to ignore him, but this proved fruitless. He would continue his repetitions, often with his voice getting louder and more urgent.

It literally took us years to figure out what this phrase meant, which was,

"Watch out, I am losing control and I am going to grab you. I need help." Although this is not a literal translation of what Ben was trying to say, it clearly contained his meaning. In his mind, "the ends" referred to the skin on our arms.

He didn't have the word "skin" in his repertoire, so "ends" represented this outside end of our body. "Pull" meant that he was about to grab our arms, dig in his nails, and "pull" our skin. He was trying to tell us that he was going to hurt us, generally because he was feeling some sort of physical or emotional pain himself. By repeating this "pull the ends" and grabbing and scratching us, he was pleading for help. How did we figure this out? By completely changing the way we looked at these "behaviors."

Instead of focusing on reinforcement, punishments, or isolated behaviors, we looked at the whole situation. We learned from reading articles by Herb Lovett, Anne Donnellan, Dan Hobbs, and others, to approach each incident ecologically. That is, to evaluate everything – the who, what, when, where of each incident, and the ABCs of each. This is a behavioral abbreviation that seeks to identify the antecedent conditions, that is, what happened just prior to the actual behavior (A), a complete description of the actual behavior that was considered problematic (B), and the consequences of the behavior occurring (C). By looking systematically at each of these, and without coloring these observations with emotions, we began to see patterns that helped us tease out understandings of what Ben was trying to communicate.

First, we realized that each of his "behaviors" – slapping, pinching, cutting, etc. was his way of trying to communicate some feeling or thought. What an extraordinary revelation for us. This was a clear declaration that Ben was a thinking, feeling person. While this may seem like "well, duh" – that is because we know so much more about autism today. When Ben was growing up in the late 1970s and well into the 1980s, behaviorism was the accepted approach for children with autism.

Even though Bob was trained as a behaviorist, he just could not bring himself to punish Ben, especially not with aversive techniques like using electric shocks or spraying noxious fumes into his face. Bob had seen these used on rats in laboratory settings. As scientist, he observed that the animal would eventually change its behavior, but he was reluctant to use these interventions on Ben. We both had also seen films of children with autism being shocked with electric stun guns and cattle prods. We had seen films of children subjected to sensory deprivation where they were made to wear helmets that obscured their vision and hearing, or where white noise was pumped into their ears preventing them from hearing anything else. We had seen children put into straight jackets to prevent them from injuring themselves, and we had seen children put in total isolation in padded small cubicles as punishment for maladaptive behaviors. Proponents of these interventions would point proudly to evidence of their success, children who did not engage in these behaviors any longer. What we often saw were highly medicated children, fearful, cowering with flat affect. We just could not do this to Ben. There had to be a better, more humane way of helping Ben. Using an approach that looked at the whole situation and what was happening for Ben held so much more promise for us.

Ben went from two years in first grade at Waters to one year each in third grade and fifth grade at Ed Smith Elementary School. Then he moved to Levy Junior High School. The kids, just as Noah had described, perceived Ben as smart. Later we were to discover their intuitions were not far off. We were beginning to see glimpses of his intellect, but then he would confound us with something that made no sense at all.

Fears and terrors

For reasons that we still don't fully understand, Ben is terrified of certain things. As a small child and well into preschool and elementary school, Ben would shriek in terror if he saw a cylindrical container like the ones used to hold Tinker Toys or Oatmeal. If the container had a shiny metal bottom, Ben's terror was almost uncontrollable. His preschool teacher would make sure these were kept safely in closets, but this was not good enough for Ben. If she needed to open that closet to retrieve some item, he would literally go ballistic.

Bars of hand soap were also a source of abject fear for Ben. Even today, with a threatening voice, he will occasionally say,

"I'll put a bar of soap in your mouth."

Who said this to him? Did someone actually put a bar of soap in his mouth? Why? When Ben was at Waters, some of the kids said they saw different adults who carried a bar of soap with them. The kids didn't know why. We could only imagine.

Rolls of clear plastic are another source of anguish for Ben. We are constantly doing home improvements, which results in frequent trips to hardware stores, and home improvement centers. It used to be that we would have to scout out which aisles held the rolls of plastic or the orange electric cords (another irritant).

"We don't need anything on aisle 7," Was the code phrase for "orange electric cords are on aisle 7" or "watch out, plastic rolls are on aisle 7."

Sometimes, however, our smugness at being pre-emptive was foiled by aggressive marketing strategies. As we successfully passed aisle 7 and, with a knowing smile, we would turn into aisle 8 only to be confronted with – you guessed it, orange electric cords or roll upon roll of clear plastic. They had been moved to a new location.

"Oh shit. We're screwed." We had to deal with it, one way or another. We quickly learned to have Penny or Sherry scout the store aisles ahead of us – giving a quick shake of the head meaning "nope, don't try this aisle." Sometimes, however, we had to go into the "devil's den" because the item we needed was located there. If one of us could go alone, that worked most often, but sometimes it just couldn't be avoided. Slowly we began to realize, too, that we could not protect Ben forever. He would have to learn how to handle situations like this. It seemed our only course of action was to figure out ways to help him through these rough experiences.

"Okay, Ben, guess what is down this aisle?" Bob would ask. It seemed that Ben already knew. We began to realize that he had outsmarted us and did know where his nemesis items were shelved. Despite knowing this, his breath would quicken and he would turn pale. His eyes would become wide and we could see the fear beginning to grip him.

"We have to go down this aisle past the orange electric cords. I need to get a new receptacle for those wires I am working on in the kitchen."

Bob's voice was soft. Ben reached out and put his hand on Bob's shoulder.

"Do you think you can handle this?" Again Bob's voice was soft, but reassuring.

"We can do this together. Does it help if you hold onto my shoulder?" As Bob posed this question, he gently put his hand over Ben's and gave a little squeeze.

"Handle it? Yes?" Ben's voice was shaky but he began to walk down the aisle. When he got to the orange cords he paused. Bob waited a few seconds, and then moved on, keeping his hand on Ben's and saying, "Look, there are the receptacles I wanted." Ben followed.

Later, as Ben got older, he would be walking with us and then suddenly disappear. It didn't take us long to figure out that he wanted to "test" himself to see if he could handle these "fears". He still does this. Most of the time he is okay. Because we frequently shopped n the same stores, and Ben also goes there now with other friends and support people, many of the employees know Ben.

"He can find that plastic stuff faster than some of our new employees." Commented one guy. Score one again for seeing Ben in a positive way.

Why do these objects frighten Ben? Who knows? Ben doesn't. We have asked him in a number of different ways, but all he ever replies is "Does it scare you? Yes?" My guess is that it has something to do with how he sees these. I have no idea what

Sue Lehr

he perceives, but I do know that like others with autism, he often perceives things differently. Maybe, instead of seeing the orange electric cords like we do, he sees the individual coils and feels threatened by them. The clear rolls of plastic must give him a very different visual stimulation or perception.

It is only within the past 5 years or so that Ben has been able to actually touch these. He will cautiously approach with his hand readied for touching, but often shivers and backs away. Sometimes he does let his fingers glance along the surface, or he delicately pinches one fold of plastic between his thumb and forefinger, lifting the roll slightly, then quickly drops it and steps back, shivering. It is a classic "approach-avoidant" response, but I seriously doubt we will ever know what is going on in his mind as he does this.

Angelo, who has worked with Ben for a few years now, knows that Ben seems compelled to go and find these rolls. Usually, however, Angelo prevents this simply by saying, "Ah, come on Ben. You don't need to go there do you?" We need a can of polyurethane. Let's get that now." Ben will give a slight smile or chuckle, as if Angelo figured him out again. They have a great relationship that is built on trust and taking care of each other.

But wait, I am getting ahead of myself. Junior high school loomed; a new building several miles away from his elementary school, new teachers, kids who would be coming from three other elementary schools, moving from class to class in crowded hallways, a different bussing schedule, and what else? We didn't know. We had already heard about some of the racial tensions and fights. We were also worried about Ben's friendships. What about girls? What was this going to be like? Could Ben handle it? Where would his support come from? Could we handle it?

Chapter 13
Junior High School

When Ben entered seventh grade in a new building and with new routines, he really had a rough time. Not only was the building new, so were his teachers and many of the kids. The schedule required Ben to move from room to room for different subjects. It was chaotic and confusing.

Unlike his elementary experiences, the two teachers paired for seventh grade did not work well together. They each had strong personalities and major control issues. Rather than trying to figure out ways of working collaboratively, they seemed to get under each other's skin. They were both young and new to the concept of teaming. They had some pretty tough kids like Ben mixed in with typical inner city kids who brought their own pieces of baggage to the milieu. It didn't take long for a sense of apartheid to exist in the room. The regular education teacher took control of the typical students and Miss Jonas had the students with autism, many of whom presented some real challenges. Ben was one of the toughest ones because he was so unpredictable. She did her best to give Ben the support she believed he needed, but the tension in the room was palpable. There were classroom aides who were to accompany Ben to different classes, but when Miss Jonas would instruct them about what kind of assistance Ben needed, or what specifically they were expected to do, often they simply refused.

"You're not the real teacher here. You're just a special ed. teacher. I don't have to do what you tell me. I've been an aide in this district for a long time. You can't boss me around. I have tenure and you don't."

These were things that Miss Jonas heard frequently. It only made her job more difficult. The district has a very strong union and these aides knew they would be well protected, especially when confronted by a new untenured teacher. They quickly informed her in no uncertain terms who was in charge. The typical kids, once again, were great. Many of them knew Ben from elementary school, and although other kids didn't, he seemed to be well liked. Kids stood up for him, protected him.

· ·

A story – Mocking Ben and the power of peers

One time, a boy who didn't know Ben started to mock him and make fun of some of his hand flapping and rocking.

Sue Lehr

"Hey, look at the retard. Ha, ha." He laughed pointing at Ben. They were in the hallway outside of the cafeteria. Some other kids were standing around. Some laughed, some hung back, hesitant. A boy from Ben's class, someone he had known at Ed Smith School stepped forward, squaring off in front of the other boy, positioning himself between Ben and other kid. He shifted slightly forward and set his hands low on his hips.

"Listen, dude. This is Ben. He's cool. We don't make fun of him, you hear me?" Although it was framed as a question, it was clear to everyone who was listening; the intended message was "back off."

A teacher who was watching this interaction and later told me about it said, "I was watching what was happening and I knew I should step in, but I just wasn't sure when or what to say. Leave it to another kid to get one up on me." Because he was Ben's friend and he cared about Ben, this kid knew what to do. I don't think you can ask for more than that.

· ·

Ben learned a lot that year about being one of the guys. It is not something adults can teach children. It has to come from the peers. My brother once told me that he believed that parents and teachers can educate our kids, but it is the other children who make them wise. I think there is some real truth in this notion. Ben learned cool things like how to walk with his hands in his pockets and how to play UNO and shoot baskets. He learned to sit on the desk and put his feet on the chair, he learned how to "hang out" and he began to feel good about himself. We saw it in his demeanor and attitude. He liked school. What a great feeling.

Eighth grade was one of Ben's best years. Mr. Willis, his teacher, was a young, dedicated, very ambitious teacher who had all the values regarding inclusion that we could ever want. Even more, he knew how to translate these values into meaningful social and academic experiences that benefited all kids.

Each morning began with some form of social activity that enabled the kids to learn about each other, their differences and their similarities. These morning meetings might revolve around board games, or dancing and music, cooking or weight lifting. Actually, weight lifting was one of everyone's favorites. Even the girls were expected to participate. This wasn't a time for competition, but it was a time to be yourself among your friends. Mr. Willis was a superb role model. He would not ask any of his students to try something unless he also tried it. He laughed a lot with his students and clearly enjoyed seeing them challenge themselves and each

Beautiful Ben

other in positive and supportive ways. It was a great way to start each morning. Regular Lives (nominated for an Academy Award documentary) showed Mr. Willis's classroom as part of the narrative on inclusion. Ben had a fleeting cameo in the film. At the end of the morning period, Ben was expected to wash his face and hands, brush his teeth, and make sure his clothes were in good order. Then he was off to his classes. The day was filled with academic classes, lunch, and personal skill development.

A story – Ben hit a baby?

I had pretty well gotten over the fear of the phone ringing, expecting some teacher or school official to tell me about some episode with Ben. Things had been going pretty smoothly and I was beginning to relax.

The phone rang, and just by the tone, I felt something was wrong. I answered cautiously.

"Mrs. Lehr. This is Mr. Lawrence, Principal of Levy." I knew who he was as soon as he said my name. I had been in many meetings with him, but his calling me "Mrs. Lehr" alarmed me. Before I could ask about Ben, Mr. Lawrence continued.

"There was an incident on a Centro bus this afternoon involving Ben."

I held my breath.

"He hit a baby."

I gasped and my mind started reeling. Ben hit a baby? I was speechless. Mr. Lawrence continued.

"Ben has violated our district policy regarding hitting and fighting. I am suspending him for two weeks."

I simply did not know what to say. Finally, I spoke.

"Is the baby okay?"

Mr. Lawrence reassured me that the baby was not injured, but that his mother was extremely distraught. He went on to say that we would receive an official letter from the district indicating when Ben would be permitted to return to school. He finished the call and hung up. I have no idea how long I held onto the phone, but I became aware that the receiver was beeping and I hung up. What happened next was a blur.

I didn't know what to do. I literally went numb. Ben came home from school. How was I supposed to question him about what had happened? How was I to take his side, defend him, explain something I could not understand myself. I literally shut down, except, I did call Ben's teacher. I was so distraught that I needed direction from Mr. Willis.

"What happened?" I asked.

It seemed simple enough. Ben had been on a community outing, a part of his IEP. He was riding the city public transit, also part of his IEP, when the incident had happened. As the bus was approaching the bus stop near the junior high, a baby on board with his mother had begun to cry. They were sitting up front near the driver. As Ben left the bus, he reached over and hit the infant. The mother shrieked and immediately Mr. Willis interceded. He quickly explained that Ben was autistic and did not mean to hurt the child. Information was exchanged and Ben left the bus with Mr. Willis. I was called shortly after this. I was terrified. Would Ben be sent back to Waters? Why had he hit the baby? We had always known that baby's crying was upsetting for Ben, but hitting a baby? That was unacceptable by any standards, including ours. What should be do?

That evening we talked to Mr. Willis again. He had talked with the mother and had tried to calm her fears. She was quite upset. The fact that Ben is black didn't help matters, either. We went to bed, feeling very disquieted. What was going to happen? We were so afraid that Ben would be kicked out of the city district, sent back to Waters, and then what? The thoughts terrified us.

We kept Ben home the next day, but after lengthy discussions, we decided we needed to meet with Mr. Lawrence. Something didn't feel right about this whole situation and we needed to explore it. We called and made an appointment for the following day. Later that day Mr. Willis called. What he had to say stunned us. It seemed that the brother of the infant who Ben had hit went to school with Ben. When his mother had described what had happened, the student had defended Ben.

"Mom, he's in my school. I know him. He wouldn't mean to hurt anyone. I'm sure he didn't mean to hurt the baby. He's autistic. He gets upset sometimes. He just can't control himself sometimes. He's a good kid."

Ah, the power of inclusion. We met with the vice principal. She had heard the defense from the fellow student and knew that the mother had reconsidered her thinking about how Ben should be dealt with. It was immediately obvious, however, that this woman was going to uphold the strict letter of the school policy about hitting and fighting. We felt doomed.

Ms. Jamison was speaking. "Under normal circumstances we would suspend Ben for two weeks. Indeed, this was our initial intention." Her voice was low and powerful. Her jaw set and her eyes were cold and piercing as she looked from me to Bob. We waited.

"It seems that Mrs. Martinez's other son, Carlos, has convinced her that Ben was not acting maliciously. He told her about Ben. He said he knew Ben from school and didn't think Ben meant to hurt the baby. She asked us to consider this in our decision about his punishment."

The word "punishment" stung me and I felt the tears welling up behind my eyes. I clenched my teeth and waited. Ms. Jamison continued.

"It is my opinion that Ben should be punished. He broke the school rule about hitting and fighting." She reiterated her decision that Ben should be suspended. I could feel the tears pushing at my eyelids.

"Don't cry!" I kept thinking. I swallowed hard and held my breath for what ever was going to come next.

"I have discussed this incident with both Mr. Lawrence and Mr. Willis. They believe that suspension would not be in Ben's best interest. As Assistant Principal, however, the decision is ultimately mine."

It was our turn to speak. We painstakingly explained that Ben would not understand that staying home was a "punishment" for something he had done to a baby on a public bus. There was a disconnect, at least for us, and certainly for Ben.

"Help us have this whole horrible experience make sense to us and to Ben." We pleaded. She listened to us earnestly, but made only one final comment.

"I will consider everything I have heard and will call you later today to inform you of my final decision." We held our breaths.

Ben's suspension was rescinded. His IEP was revised to include goals about managing himself when he felt distressed or agitated, including keeping his hands to himself, and asking for help. Was this a victory? We no longer thought this way. We had given up on trying to defeat or beat the school district. This was about Ben, not us winning or losing. We had always wanted what we thought was best for Ben, even when others had disagreed. We realized that we had become side tracked by political issues and incompetence. Having friends, peers, people who knew him was probably the very best we could ask for. It took us a while, but slowly we realized might be able to make it in the larger community outside of school. It had always been our dream for Ben and now we felt a sense of hope.

· ·

In eighth grade Ben joined a couple of after school clubs and went to a neighborhood center after school. He loved these activities especially because he could be among his peers. He didn't attend any of these activities without a lot of planning and support. His teachers and I would spend hours figuring out how Ben could participate, what kind of support he would need, and how the typical non-disabled kids would be encouraged to get to know Ben better.

One of the clubs that Ben enjoyed most was the Spanish Club. I must admit that when his teacher first suggested that Ben would enjoy this particular after school club I thought he was joking.

"Oh great," I said sarcastically. "I can just see it. Here is a kid who can barely speak English, and you want him to join a Spanish Club. You have got to be crazy."

The gentle, but slightly patronizing look I received in return made me stop. Was this another one of those examples when the adults (in this case, me) got in the way of normal, healthy interactions? I had see it happen a million times. Well-meaning adults hovering too close to the youngster with special needs, inhibiting other typical kids from approaching. Or was I guilty of over-protecting Ben, of not allowing him to have normal opportunities because I thought he couldn't handle them?

"No." I decided. The whole idea of Spanish Club was just bizarre. As if reading my mind, Mr. Willis patiently explained that the Spanish Club traditionally built a "Haunted House" as a part of the school's annual Halloween dance. For an extra $.50 kids who came to the dance could go through the Haunted House. In the afternoon before the evening dance, it was open for the neighborhood elementary students. The house was an elaborately constructed set of tunnels and booby traps, and planning and building it would be the major focus of the club's activities for the fall.

Hammering, sawing, using a screwdriver, in fact, anything related to building, these were some of Ben's favorite activities. He was good at them too. Mr. Willis knew this and saw the possibilities. Ben joined the club and the Haunted House was a huge success. Ben was one of the club members who helped sell tickets that night. He also ate lots of pizza at the party the club held several weeks later to celebrate their success.

Chapter 14

High School at Nottingham

Nottingham is a huge urban high school. The city school district is divided into quadrants and this high school is located in the southeast quadrant. It is near Syracuse University and LeMoyne College so many of the students were children of faculty and students attending these institutions. It is a multicultural school with many different languages spoken. When Ben entered Nottingham, we were told that 29 different cultures were represented in the building. We felt that Ben, with his autism, was the newest immigrant (thanks to Cindy Sutton for introducing this concept to us). We were hopeful that, like other cultures, Ben would be assimilated into the milieu and would survive.

He was assigned to Mr. Carson's room, a special education room. We were devastated. We assumed that the Integrated Autistic Program had extended to the high school too. We thought he would go into a regular homeroom and have a general education schedule just like he had in junior high, but we were wrong. "How long, how many times, how hard do we have to fight to enable Ben to be included among his peers?

It took only minutes for us to realize that Mr. Carson was clearly from the "old school" of special education teachers. Children like Ben; he saw them as children, not young adults, were very limited. According to him, they would eventually live in group homes and work in sheltered workshops. His IEPs were duplicate copies of the same goals for each student. He saw his role as maintaining peace, keeping his students calm, and never expecting very much other than compliance and good behavior. This was not what we had planned, not what we had fought for. We explained to Mr. Carson that Ben's IEP meant that he was to attend regular classes, English, Social Studies, Art and so on. He chuckled and looked at us quizzically.

"Well, you see, none of my students have ever done that, attended regular classes. That's why they are in my room. They are special education students. We work on daily living skills and prepare them for workshops and group homes." I doubt that he meant to sound patronizing, but I thought I would throw up. We appealed to the principal.

Would we have to start all over again? Fortunately, that wasn't the case. Several new young professors at Syracuse University became involved in Ben's and other similar students' academic careers. They advocated for his inclusion in regular classes and they provided training on how to have this be a successful experience for Ben, as well as his teachers and peers. It wasn't always easy. They often met resistance from teachers who didn't think students like Ben belonged in their classes. Generally, however, Ben and these professors and their graduate students won many of them over. Mr. Carson didn't protest. Before the school year ended, he announced his intention to retire.

At first, the biggest problem that Ben encountered at Nottingham was the assistant teachers. They had been used to sitting in the special education classroom all day, reading the newspaper, playing Bingo or Uno, or just hanging out. Often they took students into the community for shopping, banking, or going for a walk through a mall. It seemed like the dream job. With Ben attending regular classes, however, they were expected to take notes and support him, helping to manage his behavior and assist him with homework. They balked at this new responsibility. It meant that they had to work, and they did not like this. Some did what was expected, but others totally subverted Ben's program.

The school district hired a new teacher for Ben with Waters School District paying the bill. Ms. James was a certified speech and language therapist, new to the district and to Ben. We backed off, hoping that she was the answer to Ben's inclusion. We wanted to give her a chance, and we wanted Ben to know that we trusted that he could make it. We also knew that special education faculty from Syracuse University were there to help us, Ben and the teachers.

Facilitated Communication

In the meantime, as part of my graduate studies I was working at the Facilitated Communication Institute with Doug Biklen. After traveling to Australia and meeting Rosie Crossley, Doug had launched the Facilitated Communication Institute at Syracuse University offering training and support for people with autism and other significant disabilities to try this new communication system. As one of his doctoral students, and a Jowonio parent, I was the discussion leader of several parent groups for families who had children like Ben, children who challenged their parents in different ways, but usually behaviorally. We would talk about what our children had done (hitting, biting, smearing feces, ripping clothes, cutting, pulling hair and so on). My role was to provide a safe forum for parents to talk about how hurt they felt, how this complicated their marriages and family relationships, how their other children seemed to suffer, how they felt like others perceived them as bad parents because they could not control their children. We shared our stories, cried, hugged, laughed, but mostly gathered support from the knowledge that we were not alone in our parenting struggles.

Doug Biklen asked me to invite parents to join a new FC support group and serve as the group facilitator. I agreed even though Ben was not using facilitated communication. Bob and I had discussed it privately, but decided it just wasn't for Ben. We still thought of him as retarded. Doug asked on more than one occasion if Bob and I didn't want Ben to try facilitated communication. Bob, ever the scientist, was skeptical. He was willing to believe that this communication system worked for some children. He just didn't think it would work for Ben.

"I wasn't' sure. I saw it work for some people, but for Ben? I just didn't know how to think about this. I guess I just thought that Ben was too retarded. He didn't know how to read. How could he type? It just didn't seem plausible." We never said "no" –don't try it. We just didn't think it would work for Ben.

Ms. James, Ben's new teacher had other ideas. She wanted to try this with Ben because she had seen evidence that convinced her he was smarter than he appeared. She saw glimpses that made her think that he just might be able to read. We had not met her yet. Ben seemed to like her. It was a start. As she would later tell us, she asked Ben one day if he might like to try facilitated communication. She explained the process to him, but he typed "no" when she asked him if he wanted to try. He typed "no" – how did that happen?

Ms. James let the topic drop for a few days, only to introduce it again later.

"Ben, I really think you can do this, and I think it will make a difference in your life. Do you want to try it? We could start with some simple stuff and then go on from there. But if you don't want to, we can stop. What do you think?" Ben's response changed his life forever.

"Try it, yes." He responded verbally and held out his hand. They began simply, spelling his name, spelling the name of the town he lived in, identifying his favorite color, food, names of his friends and his sisters. Because Ms. James didn't know us and was new to the school she was not really able to verify that these answers were correct, but her gut instincts and her work with Ben convinced her that he was able to read, write and use facilitated communication.

"This is pretty cool, Ben. What do you think about telling your parents?"

Ms. James was becoming uncomfortable with Ben's facilitating without our having given official permission. She had heard all the horror stories about how demanding we were and she was fearful of starting off on the wrong foot. On the other hand, she wanted to honor Ben's burgeoning independence – he had initially said "no" so she waited. After several weeks, Ms. James asked Ben again.

"We have been facilitating now for a while" she typed, "but I am not sure why you don't want your parents to know you can do this. I don't want to get into trouble because I have not told them, and I do want to honor your wishes, so let's talk about this. Why don't you want your parents to know?" Later she told us that she only typed this. She did not read it to Ben. She waited with her hand outstretched. Ben took her hand and slowly typed.

BECAUSE MY FATHER WILL RAISE HIS EXPECTATIONS OF ME. THINK I CAN CONTROL MY BEHAVIOR. Fortunately for us, Ms. James answered simply,

"Well, I guess we will just have to see, won't we Ben?"

Learning that Ben could type, read, use facilitated communication literally changed the way we thought about him. He was right, of course, at first we expected him to calm down and not hurt himself, and be "normal." It didn't take us long to realize however that facilitated communication does not cure autism. It is simply a new form of communication that sometimes affords us insights into Ben's thinking, and at other times, totally confounds us.

Ben's fifteen minutes of fame

It didn't take long for the media to latch onto facilitated communication and its potential as a break through in the conundrum of autism. Undoubtedly, because of our friendship with Doug Biklen and our affiliation with the newly founded Facilitated Communication Institute at Syracuse University, Ben became a focus of this attention. It wasn't the first time. In his book No Pity (1993), Joe Shapiro described his first visit to Levy Junior High in Syracuse, NY. He had rightfully acknowledged that making friends and "not feeling like an outsider" (1993, p. 169) were very important to parents of children like Ben. The atmosphere in the classroom was designed to invite students from throughout the school to come in and "hang out" - and they did. They got to know Ben and the other students with autism. Many seemed to intuitively learn how to provide support and friendship, despite obvious obstacles. Shapiro quoted Luanna Meyer, then a professor at Syracuse University and a collaborator in the program design. "These [autistic] kids are ready for the world with all its complexities and the community is learning how to deal with them... We're not postponing this inevitable need to prepare these two groups of people for how to deal with each other." (p.170) Later, we learned that many people read this book and Ben's name became well known among the families in the autism network.

Two different venues thrust Ben into the limelight in the early 1990's. One was a feature article written by Mary Makarushka which appeared in the October 6, 1991 New York Times Magazine. This article featured Ben, and two of his friends, both of whom had autism: Jeff Powell and Lucy Harrison. The words they can't say" introduced the general public to the complicated world of autism and the promise of "unlocking the door to language" that facilitated communication seemed to hold. The photos of Ben by Charles Harbutt showed his concentration. Jeff was quoted as typing, "I am not autistic at the typewriter." (p. 36). Harbutt's photo of Jeff captured his sad, but pensive eyes. These photos were evocative. Makarushka's article explained a bit of the history of autism, but focused mainly on how Ben, Jeff and Lucy experienced facilitated communication and its impact on their lives. She thoughtfully explained that for Ben and for us his autism was just as confusing as his adolescence - we all had to "readjust".

The second media event that brought fame (but not fortune) for Ben was his appearance on PrimeTime Live with Diane Sawyer. This segment appeared in January of 1992. It showed how viciously Ben struggled with his autism as he sat with Diane Sawyer and his facilitator, Ms. Palmer. He could not get control of his violent behaviors. Viewers witnessed Ben rapidly slapping his neck and face, punching his head, rocking back and forth forcefully, crying out "No, Ben. No!" Diane Sawyer sat patiently, calmly, waiting for Ben to facilitate, but ultimately she had to give up. Days later, he was able to facilitate some of his thoughts about having autism (IT IS LOUSY], show his political leanings (he stated he was a Democrat), and his sense of humor. Any viewer, and we heard from many people, witnessed the tortuous actions that Ben and Jeff Powell (also appearing in this segment) endure as part of their autism. Lucy Harrison, a 15-year-old friend of Ben's and Jeff's typed about her fear of having facilitated communication taken away from her. It remains a legitimate fear.

The controversy that surrounded facilitated communication when it was introduced to the public by Doug Biklen questioned the abilities of people like Ben, Lucy and Jeff. They were not expected to be able to read, type coherent messages, express personal and unique thoughts and ideas. Skeptics accused the facilitators of manipulating these individuals, literally putting words in their - hands. They called for controlled studies, performed in clinical settings, to "prove" that the communications were independently constructed. It was a gauntlet that few families wanted to traverse; the dangers were too scary. For us, we saw it as a freedom of speech issue; that is, no one, including people like Ben, should be denied the right to communicate based on the presumption that they cannot or do not have anything to say.

A story – Just act natural

As part of the filming for Prime Time Live, a crew of videographers, lighting and sound technicians arranged to film different "family" interactions at our house. It was a Sunday early afternoon and we were having our usual family brunch. The film crew decided to set up lights, cameras, sound booms and other equipment in the middle of our ten foot by four foot antique supper table. We each were equipped with a hidden microphone.

"Just act natural," said the camera man as he and his crew literally walked up and down the middle of the table. "Keep your conversation normal." Yea, sure.

Penny and Sherry started making fun of each other in a humorous way. This was something that often happened at our table. Then they began tossing scrunched up napkins at each other. Ben, oblivious to all this commotion, sat at the end of the table (his usual spot) and continued eating. We all were laughing.

Grandad was living with us then, but this whole media attention thing was totally confusing to him. "Bob, what's going on? What are these people doing?" We couldn't help but laugh harder. How indeed do you "act natural" when four or five people are walking up and down the middle of your supper table pointing cameras in your face. Worse yet, how do we explain this to our 92 year old Grandad. Fortunately for us, viewers never saw this segment.

This public attention was exciting and mostly fun. In the back of my mind, however, a deep sense of fear and dread was growing. I was so proud of Ben, but I was becoming increasingly afraid that his birth mother would identify him and want him back. I knew it was an irrational fear, but it was there nonetheless. What would I say to her? What would Ben think? We never hid the fact that Ben was adopted, and we had always been open with both kids that they could seek to find their birth parents if they wanted, but now I was really scared that she would want Ben back, now that he was becoming famous. What if she wanted money? What if, what if??? I didn't tell anyone except Bob about my fears. He didn't tell me I was being silly, he simply said that he doubted that there was anything to worry about. Of course, he was right.

High school life was different now.

His life at Nottingham changed. Teachers welcomed him in class and appreciated his participation. He began to write and tell the other students about his feelings and life. He was given his own column in the student newspaper called "Just My Type" where he talked about his disability and what facilitated communication had done for him. He learned to facilitate with other teachers, his friends, and eventually Bob and I. It was both exhilarating and terribly frightening. We were witnessing the birth of a new son, one we had not known so well before.

Ms. James, on the other hand, was having her own problems. Because Ben was still assigned to the special education classroom, she used this as their home base. The other aides and class room assistants seemed to resent her. I am not sure why, but I can guess. With insidious ways, they began to subvert her. Someone poured hot coffee into her purse. Her jacket was 'misplaced'. Her binder of schedules and Ben's work was destroyed. These were the incidents we heard about, but we knew they were only the tip of the iceberg. To her credit, Ms. James persevered, but when the school year ended, she announced her intentions of teaching elsewhere. We could not blame her, but we were deeply saddened to see her leave. She was an excellent teacher, skilled, committed, willing to be innovative, but being young and non-tenured had made her terribly vulnerable.

Ben's next two years at Nottingham were a mishmash of people and experiences. Different teachers were hired to work one-on-one with Ben, supporting him to go to regular classes and use facilitated communication. Some of this worked, some did not. The teachers tried and I suspect Bob and I were not nearly as supportive as we might have been. We were wearing down. It seemed so simple to us. Of course it wasn't, but our focus was pretty narrow by then. Ben should be in regular classes with the necessary supports to be successful. His teachers should receive whatever training they needed to make this work. What we did not see or understand was that other people did not believe as we did that Ben had a right to be in the regular classroom. We still struggle with that.

Under the Constitution of the United States Ben has a right to be free, and under the provisions of the Individuals with Disabilities Act and the American with Disabilities Act, he has a right to a free appropriate public education and reasonable accommodations. Gee, is that so hard? Well, I guess it is for some people. I reject that notion and will fight for as long as I need to assure that Ben is not discriminated against again because he has autism. God, this sounds so noble and lofty and simple, but it isn't. I always believed that because of the Brown v Topeka desegregation decision which declared "separate is not equal", that Ben could not

Beautiful Ben

be discriminated against because of his skin color or heritage. I simply could not understand how the school could discriminate against him because of his autism. It seemed that one was the precedent for the other.

Things turn totally wretched – Ben is abused

Ben seemed to be surviving, but then things began to deteriorate. He would come home with notes from his teachers about how outrageous he had been, hurting others – Ben?? – He had hurt himself before, and us, but never other people (except the baby). He started slapping his face and clawing at his eyes and temples. He raised large welts that turned into open wounds. He was miserable and so were we. He balked at going to school, but we forced him. On more than one occasion his teacher would call and ask that we pick Ben up early.

"He's just too upset. He can't calm down."

We didn't know what was going on, but soon learned that his programming had been turned over to an assistant teacher. I didn't like him. He was big and slovenly. He always wore loose sweat pants and a baggy sweatshirt, not much of a role model for Ben and the other young black men in the school. I watched his interactions with Ben and was dismayed at how controlling he was. He would talk about Ben in his presence, as if Ben could not understand. He didn't facilitate with Ben. I raised my concerns with his teacher, but was told this is what Ben needed; someone to keep him in line. I disagreed, but felt that I could not contradict the school's interventions.

Ben's behavior deteriorated even more and we were becoming alarmed. We requested a meeting with the teachers and administrators. We arrived at the building and as we walked down the hall, I ran into an old friend who was a teacher in the building. We were in graduate school together and had known each other for years. I liked and respected him, so my face lit up when I saw him. This was a good omen.

"Hi Jim. How are you?" I could immediately tell from the look on his face that something was wrong.

"Are you here for a meeting about Gordy? This was Ben's aide who I had such concerns about.

"Yes," I answered, but my voice lacked any emotion. I just knew that something was very wrong. Jim quickly motioned me into an adjoining hallway. He looked carefully to see if we were being observed.

"Good grief!" I thought, "This is like the FBI or something from television. What the hell was going on? I didn't have to ask. Jim spoke quietly.

"Gordy was arrested today for raping his daughter. She is three. They have evidence." I heard myself sucking in my breath, gasping, gulping. I could not speak.

"You didn't hear this from me, but get Ben, make sure he is safe." He quickly hurried down the hall. A few minutes later we were ushered into the principal's office.

"Ben has made an allegation of sexual abuse against one of the assistant teachers assigned to him."

Oh, my god!!! I looked at Bob. He looked as shocked as I felt. The principal continued by telling us that after Ben's accusation, the police had been called and he was being interrogated. Ms. Palmer, his speech teacher, was with him and so was Ms. James, his teacher. Ben's accusation had been clear, graphic, and very frightening. It was awful!!!! We felt so helpless, so violated. Why hadn't they called us? Where was Ben? Why couldn't we see him? The principal answered our question without any emotion.

"You can see Ben when the police are finished interrogating him."

"Interrogating him? He is the victim here!" I wanted to scream this, but my mouth had gone dry and I simply could not speak.

The principal continued, "We knew you were coming in for a meeting about Ben, so he waited to tell you this in person." All I wanted to do was see Ben, hold him, and reassure him that he was safe. The principal explained again that the police were not finished and we would have to wait. We did. What choice did we have? I felt such a mixture of emotions; anguish for Ben, seething hatred for Gordy, and growing anger with the school for allowing this to happen under their watch. Bob and I held each other's hands while we waited. We didn't say much, but I think our thoughts were quite similar.

Later, we received a transcript of the interview with Ben. It was horrifying; disgusting, revolting. We felt cold all over and totally numb. We understood, after reading the transcript that this had really happened to Ben. He had typed in graphic detail how Gordy had abused him and how another aide (Ben identified him) had been with Gordy most of the times. He had watched. Ben said that this happened when they went to the weight room alone – ostensibly to work out or "to help Ben get control of his behavior". I don't remember much of what we were told. I was in a state of shock.

"How could this happen? How could this principal relate these events to us so devoid of emotion?" I felt my eyes filling with tears as I realized I wanted to hurt Gordy just as he had hurt Ben and his daughter. I wanted to scream. Where were you? Where were the teachers? How could this happen? Oh my God, has this man been tested for AIDS or HIV? The terror in me was like an injection of burning hot acid. What if Ben got Aids or tested positive for HIV – I couldn't think straight. I just wanted to hold Ben to comfort him, comfort me? I didn't know what I wanted to do.

Finally we were allowed to see Ben. He was pale and his eyes were wide with fear.

"Want to go home, yes?" his voice was shaky.

"Yes, Ben, we want to go home too. Let's go." We left the school and drove home in almost complete silence. Each of us had our own thoughts. We stopped at McDonald's and that seemed to focus Ben and enable him to relax. Bob and I, we needed a gallon of wine before we were able to even begin to relax. At first we were at a loss about what to do. Our first concern was for Ben. We agreed that we needed to do everything we could to assure him he was safe and that this would never happen again. We told him that we would make sure that people whom he trusted and we trusted would always be with him from now on. We praised him for his courage in telling Mrs. Palmer and the police about what Gordy and Derek had done.

"You know they are weak, bad men. You are strong." Saying this to Ben was not enough. The horrors of these episodes, it turned out there were multiple violations, have haunted Ben for years.

"What are you remembering about school?"

BEN GOT FUCKED. To this day, if he sees a man that looks like Gordy he is frightened and cowers. If he hears the name "Gordy, he tenses and looks around apprehensively. I do too.

Ralph Maurer, a psychiatrist (now deceased) who knew Ben and us through our involvement with the Autism National Committee, said that Ben was suffering from Post Traumatic Stress Disorder. We had heard of this happening for Vietnam Vets, but never for victims of sexual abuse. Times have changed, thankfully. People are more understanding and prepared, but this has not stopped people with disabilities from being abused.

We did contact a personal injury lawyer, but when he learned that Ben had made his accusations using facilitated communication he said that we would not stand a chance in court. He seemed to believe Ben and us, but was unwilling to subject Ben to the court proceedings that would basically put Ben and facilitated communication on trial. Although we were crestfallen, we had expected this. We knew no one would believe Ben, especially since he had made this statements using facilitated communication.

We don't really know what happened to Gordy or Derek. We did hear, years later, that Gordy was convicted of murder and sent to prison. I hope it was for the rest of his life.

Counseling? Would that help Ben?

We weren't sure how, but we knew our lives had to carry on. Ben didn't want to talk about his experiences, but Bob and I thought he should get counseling to help him regain his sense of strength. Bob went with Ben for weekly sessions with a gentle man who tried to be helpful, but his real interest seemed to be trying to understand how Ben experienced his autism. While this would certainly be interesting, it wasn't what Ben needed to discuss. Drawing pictures didn't help either. Having been trained as a psychologist, Bob was well aware of the techniques and strategies Dr. Postora was trying to use with Ben, and he was acutely aware that Ben was not getting drawn in. Each session became more aversive for Bob and Ben. He simply didn't want to talk about being abused. Finally, after more than two months of weekly sessions, they quit. We weren't sure what to do now except keep on going. We slowly fell back into our routines of work, school, and home life. There was an edge, however. Bob and I were acutely suspicious of any male who wanted to be with Ben. We became paranoid, fearful that he would be abused again. We tried not to be overprotective, but we just couldn't help it.

Ben seemed depressed. Going to school was torturous for him. We demanded a new teacher and threatened to sue if we did not get what Ben needed. Both school districts agreed to our demands. A new one-on-one female teacher was hired for Ben. We were comforted by the fact that his teacher would be a woman, and she seemed committed and deeply caring.

We tried to be trusting, but it was very difficult. Ms. Roberts did her best for Ben. She made new communication books and clearly expected him to use facilitated communication through out his day. She taught some of Ben's classmates how to facilitate with him, and gave them space to do this. She supported his friendships with his typical non-disabled peers in his classes and advocated for Ben's full inclusion. She made sure he was safe. Things began to settle. We were guardedly optimistic that Ben's life just might be okay again.

This can't be happening! A different allegation of abuse

"Mrs. Lehr, this is Mr. Archer, principal of Nottingham."

"Oh shit, now what?" I thought. Mr. Archer went on to alert me, confidentially, that Joey, the current assistant teacher assigned to be with Ben, had just "hot lined" Bob to the state child abuse line.

"What? He did what?" I just couldn't believe what I was hearing. Bob is a wonderful father; gentle, loving, firm, and supportive. How could Joey think otherwise? I was totally incredulous.

It seems Joey, a black male in his mid forties, had called the child abuse hot line number accusing Bob of abusing Ben. He had described how Ben had open wounds on his face, sides and arms. According to the social services investigator who visited us later, Joey had asked Ben, "Did your father hit you?" Ben had replied, "Yes."

Ben did indeed have open wounds on his face. He would cry and scratch his temples, violently slap the back of his neck, and pinch his arms, sides, and face. If we did not keep his fingernails cut short, he could draw blood and scabs would form. We kept his head shaved so that he couldn't pull out patches of his hair, which he had done periodically.

"Thank goodness, he is a boy. I don't know what we would do with a girl who does this." We tried to comfort ourselves.

In the professional literature available to psychologists, this is called "self-injurious behavior." To Joey, it was abuse by Bob.

We were stunned, numbed, incredulous, and totally pissed. How could this happen? Bob is one of the most gentle and non-aggressive people I know. Had he "hit" Ben was the question. Of course he had. If Ben put his hand near the fire or the stove burner, either of us might slap his hand and emphatically say, "No! Don't touch! That's dangerous!" Would we hit Ben to hurt him? What a ridiculous question, except when it is being asked by an investigator who had the power to take our child away. All we could think was what would happen to Ben if he were put into temporary custody somewhere else. There were no placements equipped to handle someone with Ben's needs, and even more important, we didn't want Ben to be taken away from us. We had not hurt him. Our whole lives have been dedicated to helping him have a better life. We were anxious and scared. We were also angry.

"Good grief," I told the case worker, "If we were really going to abuse Ben, don't you think we would at least try to hide the evidence? We're not stupid. We certainly wouldn't hit him where everyone could see it." The caseworker scribbled some notes on her tablet, but didn't say anything. After what seemed like an interminable interrogation, the investigator decided that Ben could remain in our home, but we would be under strict surveillance for a period of six months. We were also informed that our neighbors, friends, colleagues, and Ben's teachers would be interviewed to determine if we were fit parents. We actually found comfort in this because we knew that most people thought we were doing our best and, hopefully, they would say so.

Joey remained as Ben's aide, despite our protests. Because of Ben's experiences with Gordy, we asked our friends in the high school to watch out for Ben, protect him, keep him safe. We tried to be upstanding citizens, but felt that we were constantly being watched. We were, we found out later.

Headaches and self abuse

As the six months passed, however, we learned things that deeply distressed us. One of the first things we learned when Ben began facilitating was that he had violent headaches, probably migraines. He would gouge at his eyes and temples when these occurred. He would pinch himself, hit his arms and hands on the edges of furniture, and slap his face and neck. At first we didn't understand that he was responding to headaches. We didn't even know he had headaches. How does a non-verbal person tell you his/her head hurts? Later, Ben would tell us that he had a "stomach ache in his head". We had suspected that he might have allergies; his nose was often runny and dripping. His sinuses seemed puffy under his eyes. We asked our family doctor for a referral to an allergist.

Dr. Smith was gentle, kind and reassuring. He took blood samples, explaining that putting Ben through the traditional skin patch test would be gruesome. We waited for the results and were stunned to learn that Ben was highly allergic to all dairy products, especially milk and cheese. Dr. Smith counseled us to immediately eliminate all products from Ben's diet that contained dairy, including baked goods that contained whey or casein.

"In fact", he said, "if there is anything on the label that relates to a dairy product, don't let Ben have it." He also told us to keep chocolate and caffeine away from Ben. As soon as we learned this, we made sure everyone in Ben's school knew this also. Even his friends would help him stay away from dairy. His headaches seemed to subside and he seemed happier. He stopped hurting himself, or at least slowed down.

The allegation of abuse, however, had seemed to precipitate a new round of self abuse. We couldn't figure out what was happening. No matter what we tried, Ben persisted in hurting himself. As the six months began to wind down, Joey would tell me, in front of Ben, that he was a better father than Bob. He said that he could take better care of Ben and feed him better than I could. I became suspicious and told Mr. Archer, the principal, that I was afraid Joey would hot line us again as soon as the six month period was over. Sure enough, that is just what he did. Only this time, he accused us of starving Ben and not permitting him to have a healthy diet. He told the caseworker that Ben should be removed from our home and put in his custody. He said he could be a better parent than either of us. Because Mr. Archer had alerted the caseworker of our concerns, however, she was able to determine that Joey had been feeding Ben chocolate milk every day at lunch and other snack foods that contained cheese. Ben's self-injurious behavior was the result of his allergies to dairy, not because Bob hit him, or I malnourished him.

Our case was dismissed and we were exonerated. That did not diminish our bitterness. When would this shit stop? When would Ben be treated with dignity and respect? When would he be given a chance to just be a person, a student, a kid in school? When would weak people like Gordy and Joey stop preying on Ben because he was so vulnerable? When would other people step forward and protect Ben. When? When? When?

We believed even more strongly now that Ben belonged among his peers. His friends could keep him safe, but they didn't know what was going on. They didn't know that the teaching assistants should not be taking Ben off to the weight room or to the gym alone. We couldn't expect his friends to be his bodyguards, but what had been happening at the high school simply wasn't working. Ben was being hurt. He was receiving an academic education, however, from those classes where he was included. He tried hard to do his best and many of his friends and teachers helped him. So did some of the professors from Syracuse University. He was a freedom fighter, but he was also alone. It was very hard. Despite all he had been through, however, we still were committed to a fully inclusive experience for Ben and so was he. He wanted to be with his friends.

Should he stay in school until age 21?

Senior year is different

Ben was nearing the end of his high school career. Soon he would be 17. Legally he was eligible to remain in high school until he turned 21, but we always felt that this didn't make sense. All of his peers would be graduating when they were 18, leaving for college, work or the military. We thought he should graduate with his peers. After that? We weren't sure what would happen.

It was his senior year and another teacher was hired to be Ben's one-on-one teacher. "Doc" (that's what everyone called him, including Ben) had come highly recommended by friends and people who knew Ben. We were excited to have a certified special education teacher who we could trust and who could support Ben to become more integrated into the school culture. Doc was Ben's strongest ally and advocate. He made friends with other teachers and showed them how Ben could be included. He worked with Ben to do homework and classroom work. He made connections with other students and enabled them to appreciate Ben. He knew when to step in, and when to just let natural things happen. Because Doc could facilitate with Ben, he taught more students how to facilitate too. Increasingly, with Doc's support, they got to know Ben and he became their friend. They watched out for him, and they enjoyed him. Ben blossomed.

Ben's Just My Type column in the school newspaper gave him a forum to teach the school about him, his actions, thoughts, feelings and autism. His picture was included with each edition so everyone would know who he was. No longer could someone like Gordy spirit him off to the weight room and abuse him. Ben had a regular class schedule and was expected to attend classes and participate. No longer could someone like Joey force him to drink milk. Ben ate lunch with his friends.

Ben's friends – these were wonderful young people who became Ben's allies. They got to know him through his classes and because Doc, his teacher, facilitated friendships to develop. He gave Ben space and time to get to know his typical peers, and he helped that to happen. He knew when to be there and when to withdraw to the periphery so that true relationships and natural supports could happen. As in all high schools, a group of friends began to form themselves and Ben was part of that group. They hung out together at lunch and before and after school. The talked to each other, hugged, shared themselves, and cared about each other. They were an eclectic group of teens, males and females, gays and straights, geeks and athletes, and Ben. What brought them together? Who knows? What kept them together as a group was even more mysterious, but they were a group and Ben was part of them,

The Senior Prom – Can you believe it?

It was nearing the end of Ben's senior year. We had decided that he should graduate with his class and then spend a year of what we called "post graduate study" working on job skills and job training. In the meantime, the senior prom was rapidly approaching. The talk among the groups members was who was going and with whom. It was clear to Doc that Ben wanted to go to the prom. He wanted to ask Alisha, one of the junior girls in the group. Ben knew that Alisha had a boyfriend, but he didn't go to Nottingham, so for Ben he wasn't really a boyfriend. Probably like all young men, Ben was scared to ask Alisha for fear she would refuse. We learned about this later when Doc filled us in. Ben talked to Doc about this, and Doc gave him the advice that if you don't ask, you will never know the answer. Finally, Ben summoned the courage to ask Alisha to go to the senior prom with him – and,

and, and ---- she said "yes". Her boyfriend went ballistic. How could she go to the prom with someone else? She was his girlfriend. Alisha explained that because her boyfriend had dropped out of school she probably would never get to go to any prom, and she wanted to go to the prom. Ben was one of her best friends.

"I mean, who better to go the senior prom with than one of your best friends?" Alisha asked us. Who, indeed?

Ben rented a tux and Alisha bought a dress. Doc agreed to be the chauffeur and chaperone. We were both thrilled and scared. Doc assured us that all would be fine. We ordered a corsage from our local florist. She delivered it personally so that she could see Ben in his tux. He looked totally "studly" – tall, dark, and very handsome. Doc picked up Alisha and brought her to our house. She looked stunning and it was very evident that Ben was thrilled. Of course we took lots of photos, smiled as the tears welled in our eyes, and waved cheerfully as off they went.

"Don't wait up for us." Doc said as he closed the car door and drove off.

"You've got to be kidding!" I thought. They rolled back in around 5 AM. Ben was totally happy, but very tired. Doc looked happy and tired also, but he said it was a great evening. He was so happy to have been a part of it. I wanted to ask a million questions, but restrained myself. The next morning, actually it was the afternoon before Ben woke up I asked how the prom had been. He really didn't answer. I sort of had the feeling that he was telling me this had been his prom, not mine.

"Don't pry," my daughters told me. I didn't, but it was hard.

A few days later I ran into Pat Floyd, Ben's third grade teacher. She had watched out for Ben ever since he had left her classroom.

"Isn't that great about Ben at the Prom?" I had no idea what she was talking about. Ben had not told me anything, nor had Doc. Pat smiled sweetly.

"Ben was elected to the King's court at the Prom. He almost was elected King of the Prom. Everyone was so happy to see him there." I could feel the tears and my throat tighten.

"Wait 'til you see the pictures. He looked so cool. He clearly was a star." My son Ben, the kid with autism, a star at the senior prom, not because people were being benevolent, but because his classmates believed that he truly belonged there. He had won his place of honor.

Later, Alisha told us that some of the teachers had told her that she was so "sweet" to attend the prom with Ben. It made her angry, she said, because she felt like they were saying she was being kind in a patronizing way. She told them,

"Ben is one of my best friends and I am happy he asked me to go to the prom with him." All I could think was, "Can it get any better than this?"

Ben graduates from high school!

The end of the school year was rapidly approaching; tests, final papers, performances and graduation practices. Doc insisted that Ben participate in all of these. We all agreed that Ben would "walk the stage" with whatever support he needed. Graduation was to be held in a local historic theater. We got Ben there to meet Doc who whisked him off to get his cap and gown. We found our seats. Penny was with us and our friend Pat Floyd joined us.

"I am not going to miss this graduation for anything." She shouted above the voices of the crowd. The theater was crowded and we had to sit quite far back on the ground level. Doc had told us which side to sit on, however, so that we could see Ben as he walked down the aisle toward the stage. Hundreds of seniors were graduating. Their names were called in alphabetical order. They had to walk up to the stage, cross part way and shake hands with the senior class advisor, move on to the principal who handed each student their diploma, and then move on to the superintendent who would shake the student's hand before he/she could leave the stage. Could Ben make this journey? Would he be able to shake hands, not lose control, carry the diploma? I was terrified he was going to totally fall apart. The trip down the aisle was tense. He walked holding onto Doc's shoulder and the student behind him periodically rubbed his back. As he approached the stage, I held my breath.

"BEN LEHR" the announcer's voice resonated loudly and clearly throughout the auditorium. There was a brief hush. Ben stepped onto the stage with Doc close behind. He walked quickly to the principal and accepted his diploma. Suddenly, the entire senior class sprang to their feet and began applauding for Ben. Everyone around me stood up and began applauding. I couldn't see what was happening. I tried to scramble up to stand on the seat, but by that time, Ben had shaken hands with the superintendent and was briskly heading off stage. Everyone in the auditorium seemed to be clapping for Ben, at least it seemed that way to me. I was totally overwhelmed with pride for Ben. I also felt deep emotions for his classmates who understood what this meant for Ben. It was, according to Penny, "totally awesome."

Later, after the ceremony, we met Doc and Ben outside the theater. They were grateful to be able to rid themselves of their caps and gowns. It had been hot and they were sweating. I knew this was nerves also, but I didn't care. I hugged them

Beautiful Ben

both and told them how deeply proud I was of both of them. I think I was blubbering, but nobody made fun of me. Penny was telling everyone who passed by,

"This is my brother. He just graduated. Isn't that great?" Ben handed her his diploma and we all went on chatting about the ceremony. Suddenly, Penny said,

"Ben, Mom, Dad, look at this." She was holding Ben's diploma.

"It's a real diploma! Mom, Ben, look!! It's not an IEP one." She was jumping up and down. We looked – carefully. Penny was right. It was a real diploma.

"Oh my God, how could this have happened?" I quickly began thinking about what might happen. Had Ben really completed all the necessary requirements for graduation? Wasn't he supposed to receive an IEP diploma? Could the school district have made a mistake? Could they strip Ben of this diploma? What should I do? What should I do? Bob came to the rescue.

"Ben just graduated. Let's celebrate that." Leave it to Bob to state the obvious. Later we could worry about the "real" diploma. For now, this was Ben's moment to shine. Many of Ben's classmates swept by sporting their caps and gowns, laughing, shouting with joy. Many also stopped to say,

"Way to go, man!" Or "Hey Ben, congrats!" or "We did it, Ben. We graduated!" We hugged, kissed, and jumped up and down. This was such a great night!! All of our fights, our hurts, our frustrations, our pain, had come to this. Yes, it had been worth it!! Our battle scars ran deep, but not for Ben. He was proud, happy and a graduate. We went home to celebrate.

Chapter 15

Work, Volunteering, and Entrepreneurship

After Ben graduated from high school, we were faced with the dilemma of what should he do each day. We decided to opt for one more year of high school, although we called it his "post graduate" work. Ben had been volunteering at a local community college library and he wanted to continue this, which we thought was a good idea. He liked being among the students and fairly quickly got into the routine of what was expected. Ben's main responsibility was to collect the returned books that had been deposited in various locations around campus. If the weather wasn't too ghastly, this was a good time. Once back at the library he had to help re-shelve the books that had already been returned and sorted. This was more difficult because he was supposed to distinguish the different bar code numbers so that the books were re-shelved in the right locations. Usually, he ate lunch in the campus cafeteria. He often saw kids he had gone to school with and he liked that. This was a difficult job for Ben, requiring him to stay focused and on task. He did the best he could, and he liked being given the opportunity.

And so, as Ben was nearing graduation, we met with the district's transition team to figure out how this experience could be continued and potentially lead to real employment. They referred Ben to the local vocational rehabilitation office for evaluation and follow-up. We thought they should have contacted the library to determine Ben's abilities and what opportunities he might have for a real job. Since this didn't happen, we assumed that was what the vocational counselor would do eventually. Waiting for the state agency took time and there always seemed to be some sort of bureaucratic hurdle. This really frustrated me. Having met with the school's transition team led me to believe this was going to be a smooth transition. It wasn't, and time passed. When Ben finally finished the school year in late June, nothing was in place.

Because we saw this coming, Bob and I developed our own "work" plan for Ben. We didn't want Ben to lose his routine and relationships, so we set about finding different people, usually college students, to work with Ben at the library. We paid them out of our own pockets. Sometimes these students would provide transportation for Ben, but that wasn't always possible. This was a scheduling nightmare and a new financial burden.

By then, Ben had a service coordinator whose responsibility was to work for Ben, finding the services he needed in the community. I had met Brad when I was teaching at Syracuse University. He was a graduate student in Vocational Rehabilitation, and was working at a local human service agency as a Service Coordinator for people with disabilities. He had met Ben on several occasions and they enjoyed each other. I liked Brad because he was calm, gentle, and had a strong commitment to seeing folks like Ben be employed in meaningful jobs. He approached the library staff about a part time paid position for Ben. He also investigated the possibility of Ben becoming a part time college student. While these negotiations were going on, I tried to keep Ben's schedule stable. This was a nightmare. I spent hours on the phone, scheduling people to support Ben at work or to make sure he had a ride to the college and back. What frustrated me the most, however, was I really had no idea if Ben was doing okay. We got no feedback from the library staff, and the support people were pretty uncommunicative. Brad tried to do some oversight, but he became frustrated by the lack of interest in Ben's welfare on anyone's part. As hard as we all tried, it just never seemed to work. The college students had conflicts of their own, or they would get full time jobs, or they quit for one reason or another.

To make matters even more complicated, the vocational rehabilitation process seemed stalled. They required Ben to go through a battery of vocational tests, mostly unrelated to his work in the library. To me, it seemed like such a waste of time, especially since he would have to miss work to complete these. Another problem was that the vocational counselor assigned to "Ben's case" told us that she doubted that Ben would be deemed eligible for job coaching services because of the severity of his disability. This just didn't make sense to me. The state's vocational services were intended for people with disabilities. How could Ben be rejected? He was; mainly because there was no expectation that someone with autism could have "a real job." People like Ben were expected to be grateful to get a placement in a day treatment center or, at best, in a sheltered workshop.

"You know, Mrs. Lehr, the waiting lists for these placements are quite long and it will take Ben months, maybe even years, to get in. You really need to get his name on the list as soon as possible." I couldn't believe my ears. He already had a "placement" at the library, if you wanted to call it that.

"Can't you help Ben there? He doesn't need to go through vocational evaluations and stuff like that. He has a job. Why can't you help him with that?" I was repeating myself, but I was getting so frustrated.

"Penny, Ben's sister, would like to help him, but she needs to be paid. Would that be possible?" I could tell from the look on the counselor's face that this was never going to happen. What made this so maddening to me was that this counselor and I had worked together at another agency, before she took this job. I had served on advisory boards for the state vocational rehabilitation office and knew the director well. For years before Ben graduated I had told them about Ben and our desire for him to be employed in a regular job. He was not going to go to a sheltered workshop or a day treatment center. We had worked too hard to keep him in an inclusive setting in high school to have him end up here. Placement in a day treatment center, however, was the only option offered, and that would probably be months away.

"No! You do not have our permission to put his name on that list."

Meanwhile, Brad learned that the library was not in a position to hire Ben because it was administered by the county and involved civil service employment.. Any part time employees were actually work-study students attending the college. This was going nowhere.

The whole idea fell apart when Brad and his wife decided to move out of state. We would have to find a new coordinator which would take time. I was still trying to hold things together, but the supervision of the support people, hiring, firing, spotty transportation, it all just was so complicated. Bob and I kept trying and so did Ben, but it fell apart.

We have to do something different.

We gave up. We told the library staff that Ben wouldn't be coming back. They didn't respond at all. It was sort of sad and anticlimactic. With help from the Employment Coordinator of a local human service agency, Ben volunteered again in hopes that this might lead to some other kind of job. Briefly, he volunteered at a food bank, but it was a disaster. He hated it. Then he and Bob spent some time volunteering for Habitat for Humanity, but that didn't work out well either. We were trying to coordinate everything, which meant there was no consistency and no coordination. Nothing seemed to lead toward real employment. Friends tried to help, but none of us knew which way to go. In retrospect, we realize that we were trying to plug Ben into a traditional work model and he just was not a traditional worker. It took us a long time before we could recognize this and begin to ask Ben what he wanted to do.

Ben tried college

Over the years, Ben has said that he wanted to go to college - to study English and writing. He tried auditing a course at the community college, but could not get into the class he wanted. The only open class was Biology and Ben's service coordinator registered him. I am not sure how that course was decided upon, but I suspect it was because the professor was willing to give Ben a try. It didn't work. No one was expected to attend class with Ben, give him support, and help him negotiate the campus and the schedule. Ben missed a lot of classes. Once again, we tried to piece things together and, once again, it just didn't work. Finally, it was obvious that Ben just could not remain still and quiet during the lectures. He didn't want to be there, but we still didn't understand that we weren't listening to his desires. We were trying to fill his day by scheduling things he didn't want or could not do. We were not listening to Ben. We kept trying, however, thinking that we were doing the right thing.

Many years later, Ben tried college again. It just wasn't a good fit for him then either. I wondered if part of the reason he agreed to try college level work in the first place, was for us, his college professor parents.

Now, what to do?

Ben was getting depressed. We were getting frustrated. It was time to stop and take a breath, regroup, rethink.

Ben typed, SHOULKD HAVE LIBRARY JOB BUT (they) KEPT ME
FROM WORKING AT THE LIBRARY. MEANT THAT I HAD TO
FIND SOME THING NEW. LOOKED (at my) GIFTS. SUTDIED
MY SELF. MY GIFT. STUDIED GREAT THINGS. COULD WE
HELP KOOL PEOPLE TO STAY JUST CALM. BUT GIFT IS
PEOPLE WHO TRY TO HELP ME MAKE FRIENDS. GIFTS
MEANS WHAT I THINK I CA N GIVE TO OTHERS. JOKE. GIFTS
ARE FRIENDS AND BEING RESPECTED.

"Ben, if you could do anything you wanted, what would it be?" Bob, Ben and I were sitting around our supper table, a constant place for family, fun, food, and sincere problem solving.

WANT TO WORK WITH POWER TOOLS. YES?

"You what?" Should I clean my ears? Had I heard him correctly? One look at Ben and I knew he had just told us what he really wanted to do. Later I would wonder how long he had been thinking this, waiting for us to ask. Bob and I just sat there. My mind was whirling and I knew Bob's was too. For years we had been rebuilding our old house, making book shelves, laying hard wood floors, shingling the outside with cedar shakes, paneling the living room with cherry boards, hanging rough sawn cedar as the ceiling and so on. Ben had been part of each of these projects, as we called them. He had always loved to hammer. For years, before we had rebuilt our front porch, Ben had an old stump that he loved to hammer. We would give him odd pieces of left over wood, or broken shingles, a 100 lb. box of nails, a couple of different sized hammers, and he would pound away. We called it his sculpture. It didn't take him long to begin to hammer nails into the porch floor and walls, but we didn't care. Eventually, we planned to tear it all apart and extend our living room. Working with power tools, however, was totally different from using a hammer. It was certainly more dangerous.

"Okay, Ben. Let's think about this. I could probably teach you how to use different tools, but you would have to really commit to this. You would have to learn safety measures, be careful, and not get agitated." Bob spoke calmly, but Ben and I knew he was being sincere.

"Good grief!" I thought. "He is really going to try this with Ben. He's being serious." Then, I realized Ben was serious also. He had never been afraid of the loud noises. In fact, he seemed to get excited, happy, when Bob was using the radial arm saw or his electric drill. Ben would often gently place his hand over Bob's. It was worth the try. Bob was continuing to speak.

"Let's try this for six months. I'll show you how to use my tools safely. We'll have to decide what to build. If it works okay, then we can decide what to do next." Ben smiled.

TOOLS YES.

Such a simple statement, but it seemed like we had just crossed an important threshold. We finally had asked Ben what he wanted - how simple. Why hadn't we done this before? And so we began, or at least Ben and Bob did.

Bob showed Ben how to use each piece of equipment in his shop. He found that Ben was an eager learner. Bob would demonstrate the proper way to use the tool, telling Ben just what steps he needed to be safe and successful. We both knew that too much talking was not good for Ben so Bob told him just what he needed to know.

"Hold the handle like this. Keep your other hand over here away from the blade. Pull the saw slowly and carefully." They were working with the radial arm saw.

Beautiful Ben

Ben refused to wear the safety goggles so Bob abandoned that practice. He stood beside Ben, placing his hand over Ben's, pulling the blade forward. Next, he moved his hand to Ben's wrist, then his forearm, his elbow, his shoulder, his back. With each pass of the blade Bob withdrew more and more of the support so that finally Ben was able to pull the saw blade independently. In between passes Ben would occasionally "spaz" or bop up and down. When his hand was on the saw handle, however, his movements were controlled and careful. His look was intense.

Bob methodically showed Ben how to use each tool by teaching each step that was needed for safety and completion. He talked Ben through each step. Later, when Ben was able to do things fairly independently Bob would ask him, "What should you do first? Where should you put your hands? What's next? That's good. What do you need to do now?"

Sometimes Ben would answer him, but generally he simply did the next step. Finally Bob felt they were ready to make something, a real product. I had just had foot surgery and needed to keep my foot elevated. Bob and Ben agreed that they would make a footstool for me. They had already made a couple of simple bird feeders, but the footstool would be more complicated.

"After working with Ben for a few months I knew what he could do well and what he liked to do. Finish work, staining, painting, applying polyurethane was not his thing. He was sloppy. He just didn't seem to have the fine motor skills, or the interest in doing this. He loved sanding, using the planer, sawing with the radial arm saw, things like that. He got really good at these. So we made our first table. We used pine to make a mission style stool. I had read about different kinds of joints so we decided to try biscuit joints. Later we used mortise and tenon joints because they were stronger and Ben liked making these. With the biscuit joints, he didn't like putting on the glue and we often had large drips down the legs. It was really messy." We still have this first table in our living room. We all agreed Ben had found his "gift." He could turn this gift into a business.

I bought a book about how to start your own business while Bob and Ben began making more tables. By this time, Ben had moved out of our house and was living in his own home. He and Bob built a small shop in the basement. Since Bob was busy teaching, he let Ben borrow some of his tools. We asked the agency to help us find other people who might be able to work with Ben. In the meantime, Penny offered to fill in. She had been doing construction work, roofing, and restorative masonry, but with a two-year-old daughter and another baby on the way, working with Ben was a much better option. He was flexible about her hours. She had the skills needed to support him in his work, and they liked working together.

MY WORK IS MAKING WOODEN TABLES. I LIKE PEOIPLE DOING
   PRETTY PRESNTS. JUST LIKE MAKING THINGS.

MY SISTER JUST LIKES TO WORK WITH ME. UPSET WHEN
   SHE IS SI CK. WHERE I GET HELP FROM PENNY IS TO GET
   THE TOOLS FUNCTIONING - LIKE THE RADIAL ARM SAW
   WHEN IT NEEDS ADJUSTING. TOOLS I USE ARE TENON AND
   MORTISE MAKER AND ORBITAL SANDER.

MY SHOP IS IN THE BASEMENT LOVE TO HAVE MY SHOP IN
   THE BARN AT PENNY'S HOUSE. JUST THINK THAT IT WOULD
   BE NICER IF I HAD MORE ROOM.

NOT ENOUGH ROOM NOW.

LOOK HOISE IS OKA. BUT JU ST TOO TINY. GREAT TO BE
   ABLE TO KILL MORE THINGS AT ONE TRIME THAT NEED
   FINISHING.

We applied for a business license and Ben Lehr and Company became a reality.
Of course, the "company" consisted of Bob, Penny and I. Over the subsequent years
other people have helped in one way or another. The main problem we have had is
finding someone to work with Ben on a sustained basis who has the requisite skills
and knowledge for this type of work. Even more important, Ben needs someone who
is not going to be intimidated by the power tools or his autism. This is truly a unique
combination. How do you put that into a job description? Different people were hired;
some had the skills and the commitment, but were inadequate in some other way.
For example, Ben was pretty clear that he no longer wanted to make bird houses
or bird feeders because he felt these were things made by less skilled people. He
is very proud of his work and relishes the positive comments people make when
they see his tables. Nevertheless, whether it was because the worker was afraid
of the power tools himself or of Ben and his autism, he still ended up making more
and more birdhouses and bird feeders. If you asked him, however, he would tell you
he wanted to make tables. Of course we knew this, but we could not compel the
support workers to do what they thought was risky or dangerous to them or to Ben.

Years later, when his home was destroyed in a fire, Ben lost most of his work.
The tools were not damaged in the fire, but now he had no place to work. The
agency that supported him in his home, stepped forward and found a local church
that had a large space where Ben could set up shop, at least temporarily. It was

quite a distance from home. The Vocational Services Coordinator would pick Ben up in the morning and take him to work. This was his church. We didn't know much about it, but he explained that there were other programs being run in the building and Ben would be sharing space with the teen theater group. He and Ben set up the tools, arranged their wood, and tried to get back into production. Besides working with Ben and doing his other duties, the Coordinator was placing ads for a new person to work with Ben.

We had all agreed to do our utmost to keep Ben's life as consistent as possible, given the fire and the resulting chaos, but it just couldn't be done. There were too many complications. We were trying to negotiate building Ben a new house and Ben wanted a real shop this time. So did we. The new house that was being built was on a large piece of land that we already owned. Penny had lived there with her boyfriend when he was killed. There was an old barn near the house so we began to investigate what we would have to do to convert it into a shop for Ben. We had already put on a new roof, but the foundation was crumbling, the siding was old and deteriorated. The best estimate for stabilizing and repairing the foundation walls was over $25,000. Then there was the electrical work needed, insulation, windows and on and on. The more we talked about what needed to be done the more we realized that we would be better off building a new shop. Later, if we wanted to restore the barn we could. Since we had taken out a home equity loan in order to build the house, we decided to dip into this to build the shop too. The combination of the proceeds from the sale of the Lancaster House, after it was fully restored, and the home equity line of credit afforded us the cushion to do this. In the meantime, we still needed someone who could work with Ben and do it right. We were beginning to wonder if this person actually existed. He did!! But first, Ben needed a real shop or at least enough space for his tools.

When he moved to his new home, over six months later, Ben's state-of-the-art wood shop was build right next door. It was a large 28 x 32 feet building, with picture windows overlooking the fields and mountain behind Ben's property. We moved all of Ben's tools there and some of Bob's. There were different workstations, places to store wood and supplies, an exhaust system, even a bathroom. It was well lighted and had a heated floor. Ben loves to spend his time working in his shop.

Welcome Angelo

Angelo was hired over four years ago. He is an artist whose work has involved ceramics, metal sculptures, painting, photography, marble work, and yes, woodworking. Hooray!! He wasn't that experienced with people with autism, but he had worked with troubled teens and people with other kinds of disabilities over the years, so Ben did not intimidate him. Penny and Bob showed him how they each worked with Ben, but Ben was really the instructor. He and Angelo began to adjust to each other as their friendship developed.

Angelo arrives every weekday around 7am. He and Ben have breakfast together and plan the day's work. They take breaks as Ben needs them, but stick to the general routine of working until lunchtime. After lunch they are back at work until around 3pm. There are days, however, when Ben is out of sorts and he simply cannot or will not work. His body seems to be out of control and he seems unable to regain the appropriate balance to be safe and productive. Some days they go to the local home improvement center to get some supplies. In the summer they make a weekly trip to the farmer's market for lunch and some down time. They have also planted a huge garden with vegetables and flowers. In the late summer, they reap the benefits of fresh organic food - Ben especially loves the tomatoes, broccoli and cauliflower. Last year, the sunflowers grew to over 10 feet. They work every day and Ben is happy because he is productive and valued for his work.

Selling his product at craft shows.

In the beginning we arranged for Ben to sell his tables at a Regional Market, and then later in local craft shows. We had no idea what we were doing, having never tried this before, but it was fun. When he sold a table we were ecstatic. The shows were arduous work, however. The day before a show, Ben, Bob and I would go to Ben's shop and load up his tables into our old truck. We gingerly wrapped each piece in old blankets to prevent scratching. I would prepare my "work box" as I called it. Actually it was an old milk crate loaded with our money box, a calculator, pens and pencils, price tag stickers, tape measure, fliers and brochures we had made up about Ben and his work, furniture polish and soft cloths, suntan lotion, band aids, aspirin, tissues, paper towels, scissors, and, of course, toilet paper. We bought a pop-up canopy that we would struggle to erect, forgetting each time what sequence of set up steps was needed. This canopy was great for keeping off the beating sun or the rain. Our canopy was 10 feet by 10 feet, the size of most of our sites. We would bring along folding camp chairs so we could sit in the back of the site with Ben's tables in the front. We also packed a cooler with sodas and water, lunch, and snacks. We brought rain parkas, extra sweatshirts, and something to read.

The night before a show Ben would usually spend the night at our house because we had to be up early to get to the check in station, get to our site, set up and be ready for what we hoped were going to be the buying hordes of people. We learned quite quickly that even though the show is advertised to open at 10 AM, many prospective customers were there much earlier. I guess they wanted to beat the crowds. We also learned that just because the craft show organizers said the show would close at 6 PM or 7PM, many people would still be milling around looking for bargains or new people would arrive late not realizing that we were exhausted, dirty, and eager to close up.

In the beginning we weren't sure if Ben would be able to stay through a whole day, but it soon became clear that we had underestimated him. He loved the shows, especially when people would comment on the fine workmanship. Invariably they would look at Bob and compliment him.

"Oh, that's my son's work. He builds these tables. We're just here to help." And Bob would point to Ben. The reactions were mixed. Most people would look at Ben, ready to say something, and then, just for an instance we could see the shock flash across their faces. We generally waited for what ever came next. Some people would look down, certainly confused, possibly embarrassed, unsure of what to say or do. Some walked away without saying anything. Some lingered, looked around at the tables, picked them up or swept their fingers over the smooth surface.

"You did this? You made these? This is really good work. What kind of wood is this? How did you make these? This is good craftsmanship. Do you take orders? I need a table for my living room, but I am not sure of the size. Do you have a website?" These were the questions and comments we loved and which Ben relished. We developed a routine. Generally, I would talk to the customers. Bob has never been the social one in our family. Ben just liked to sit and watch the people and listen to what they said. Men usually wanted to talk to Bob about how the legs were joined, or what kind of tools Ben had used. We put tags on each table detailing the kind of wood, oak or cherry (Ben stopped using pine because very few people wanted that), and the dimensions.

We also displayed the price prominently. People often commented that Ben's tables should be more highly priced. That was a compliment all by itself. I would explain that Ben was not doing this to make money. He wanted to work and loved making the tables. The prices usually covered the cost of the materials and that was enough. We wanted people to buy them, not just look.

Taking orders caused too much pressure

For a while we also took orders, but we stopped when we began to realize that this was putting a lot of pressure on Ben to "get something finished and delivered."

He is not a fast worker and pressure like this only made him uncomfortable. Angelo didn't like it either.

One particular order was what convinced us of this. It was before Angelo started working with Ben, but we thought we could fill it. Ben had been selected to be in a local show, a three-day show that was juried. One section of the show, which drew thousands of people, had been designated for local artists only. He had submitted photos of his work because one of the people who worked with him, a potter, thought he should. He was accepted. He was the only wood worker in the show. We were bursting with pride, but we had no idea what we had gotten ourselves in for. Most of our shows had been one-day events. This one started on Friday morning and ended at 6 PM on Sunday. One of the challenges, among many, of a show of this nature is to be sure you have enough products to sell. We set it up that, if needed (hopefully), Bob could get to our truck and drive to Ben's house to get more tables.

Fortunately, the weather was spectacular and the attendance at the show was huge. We had a good site and the crafters on either side of us were fun and very helpful. Three full days, however, of meeting and greeting people was exhausting. We had to laugh at some of the comments or questions people asked.

"What is this?" a person would ask, pointing to a table.

"Well duh." was my thought, but never my reply.

"I guess it depends upon what you might need it for." I smiled sweetly. "It could be an end table, a foot stool, maybe a child's step stool. What are you looking for?"

Of course, there would be those who stopped, looked, stroked the table, picked it up, turned it over, asked questions or just chatted, but then moved on. It was always hard to determine if we should engage them, or wait for them to initiate a conversation. Sometimes I would simply ask "Can I answer any questions for you?" Invariably I would do this if someone came back to look at something again. I would wait, standing back, before I would say anything. On the second day of this particular juried show a well-dressed older gentleman and his wife stopped. They looked, asked some routine questions, and then stepped back and chatted with each other before they moved on. Later that day, they came back.

"Does he take orders?" the man asked.

"Well, it sort of depends on what you have in mind." I wasn't going to mislead this man into thinking Ben could do more than he could.

"Well, I have some hand painted ceramic tiles that my son brought back from a trip. They're quite lovely. We were going to have the mounted on a wall in our house. I saw these tables, however, and I began thinking of how nice it would be if the tiles could be inlaid in the top of something like this one." He pointed to a solid oak end table.

"I think it would need a shelf below. Could he do that?" Ben had built tables like what this man was describing, but never with the inlaid ceramic tile top.

"Let me talk to Ben and my husband about that." I looked at Bob who was definitely skeptical. Ben was oblivious.

"I'm pretty sure we could do that, but it would take time." I wondered as I said it if I was promising something we could not produce.

"Well, we would want two of them. Matching each other." He looked at me expectantly.

"Ben builds things one piece at a time. He would do his best to make two tables match, but there might be slight variations. He would do his best."

"I'll measure the height of what we want and call you next week. We can arrange to meet so that you can get the tiles."

How much would something like this cost?" Mr. Bonner was stroking the top of a cherry table.

"Well, to be honest, I am not really sure. Let me talk with Ben and the person who works with him. When you call me next week, I can give you a price." I had no idea what I was doing and I could see Bob looking frustrated. The man gave me his name and left.

"It shouldn't be so hard to build this, um - these tables, should it?" I look hopefully at Ben and Bob. They both looked back blankly. They had no idea if Ben could do this. There were other customers. We needed to move on. Finally the show was over.

We were exhausted, but also elated that Ben had done so well. The comments about his workmanship were positive, thrilling, and the number of tables that he sold - well, he almost sold out. It was a beautiful feeling, but then reality arrived with a phone call from Mr. Bonner. He wanted to arrange a time to deliver his hand painted tiles so that Ben could build two oak tables with the tiles inlaid on the top and a shelf located beneath. I agreed. I am not sure why I thought this would be easy, but I did. I thought Bob could help. I didn't realize that his Alzheimer's would rear its ugly head in the form of depression.

We all worked on these tables. I met with Mr. Bonner and received the tiles - 3" square, boxes of them. He explained that they had each been hand painted in Mexico and that his son had bought them as a gift for Mr. Bonner.

"If I decide to move, I can take these tables with me." It was a simple statement, but I understood the importance of it.

"We'll do the best we can, Mr. Bonner. I think it will take about 2 months to make these. I'll call you and let you know about our progress."

"You'll be careful with these, won't you?" I realized he was afraid to let them go. Each tile had been carefully wrapped in newspaper and then lovingly placed in a sturdy cardboard box. I could feel his emotions crowding his rational need to have these tables.

"Of course, we will be very careful. I promise. I'll call you." As I loaded the boxes of tiles in the trunk of my car I realized he was having doubts about what he had just done. We had met in a parking lot half way between his house and ours. I waved confidently, and drove away. I was beginning to have second thoughts myself.

Bob, Penny, Dee (her boyfriend) and Ben's support people all worked on creating the model. A prototype was made but it was awful. The bottom shelf was too low, way too low, the workmanship was sloppy, and they hadn't figured out how to lay the tiles securely. Ben had worked on these two tables for weeks. I wondered if he realized that they were pieces of junk. By this time, two months had gone bye. I had to call Mr. Bonner and tell him what had happened.

"If you want us to, we can return your tiles. I know you have been waiting patiently, but we just did it wrong. I am sure Ben can make these, but we have to start over. It will take time." I could hear the frustration in his voice.

"I wanted to have these to show to my son when he visits next month. Do you think you can have them by then? Can you promise me that?"

"No, Mr. Bonner. I can't promise anything other than Ben will do his best." I waited almost hoping he would tell us to forget the whole thing. Bob and I had been at odds about this whole project from the very get go.

"I don't want to do this. I can't help Ben with this. Send the tiles back. Who cares anyway?" I should have realized the pressure and stress I was creating, but I didn't.

Penny and Dee stepped in and totally rescued the whole project. Penny helped Ben construct the tables and Dee laid the tile. The tables were beautiful. We were so proud of Ben, and of Penny and Dee. I called Mr. Bonner and made arrangements for the delivery. He wanted them delivered to his house and I agreed. It was really anticlimactic. Mr. Bonner was not there. His wife greeted us at the front door and showed us where we should put the tables, in the kitchen.

Beautiful Ben

"Thanks. How much do we owe you?"

"That was it? I thought. No comments, no acknowledgement that this was fine work? I gave her a flier about Ben. She gave me a check and showed us the door. That was it. I am not sure what I expected, but I think I wanted some recognition that Ben's work was good. After all the work, the stress, the angst, nothing - just a check. Maybe my expectations were too high. I was so glad that we had not taken Ben with us. What a downer that would have been for him and us. After that we decided that orders were not worth the stress. We did do a couple, but the circumstances were different, but that was the end. Our venue from now on would be craft shows.

Are craft shows the right venue?

This wasn't such a good plan either. I liked doing the shows, talking with people, schmoozing with the other crafters, seeing Ben praised for his work. Bob, however, found these times gruesome. He participated, but he hated it. He would sit in the back of our little 10 x 10 display area and read the newspaper. One particular local show, he enjoyed because he knew many of the people who stopped by our booth. It was like old home week and we could visit, chat, and catch up with each other. The other shows and all the preparations for them, was just too much. It didn't take me long to realize this was not working. Our last show - clinched it.

We got to the street where the show was to be held and I jumped out of the van to check in and find out where our booth was located. I had been driving; I ran across the street to check in, but when I looked back at the van I could see that Bob looked confused. He was not well and I was afraid this might be too much for him, but I wanted Ben to be successful too. I felt torn.

I waved reassuringly and mouthed, "I'll be right back. I checked in, feeling impatient and anxious. I kept watching the van for signs of trouble. I got our check-in materials and sprinted across the street.

"Okay, we are all set. We have a space close to where we were last year." I smiled and threw the van into gear.

"Where were we last year? I don't remember being here." Bob said innocently.

"Well, let's look for S-17 - it should be chalked on the sidewalk." We found it and unloaded the van.

"Here Ben, you take this table and put it over there." Bob was taking out the canopy, chairs, and other paraphernalia. I could see he looked confused and stressed. I tried to slow down and make it fun, but I knew I wasn't succeeding. We unloaded and began to set up the canopy. This has always been a challenge, mainly because we never took the time to figure out which step came first and so on. I had been worried about this so I had gotten out the directions to be sure we could do it successfully, but we still messed it up.

No matter what we tried to do, the canopy would not open. The crafters next to us tried to help, but it just didn't open. I was getting anxious and I could tell Ben and Bob were at their breaking point. This definitely was not fun.

"Oh my god, Bob. Look! The top is caught on that street sign and on that tree branch. No wonder we can't open it." We looked up and saw that the top of the canopy was jammed under a street sign on the one side and caught on an overhanging tree branch on the other. We stood on our overturned milk crate and released the canopy from under the sign. On the other side, Bob got up onto one of Ben's tables and simply broke off the offending tree branch. The canopy was free and we opened it. The show hadn't even started and I was exhausted and drained.

It turned out to be a fabulous show. Ben practically sold out of everything we had brought. Once again, the weather had been spectacular and the people had been generous and gracious about Ben's work. By the time we packed up, however, around 7 PM, we were drained. It had been a long day and I knew it had been our last as craft show participants. It had become too hard for all of us in one way or another. As if to confirm my thoughts, I heard Bob's exhausted voice.

"I can't do this again. It's too much for me. I just can't do this again." I choked up, but tried not to let the tears show. I vowed to never put so much stress on Bob again.

"I love this man. Why the hell am I making his life so much harder." I was ready to beat myself up, well, at least emotionally, when Ben asked to go to McDonald's on the way home. It snapped my "feeling sorry for myself" mood. I needed to think about Ben and Bob.

"Sounds good to me." Of course, what I really wanted was a huge glass of wine. That would come later.

Creating a show room

As we got to know Angelo he told us he was searching for a studio where he could work on his own art. He needed space especially where he could sculpt large metal pieces - 6, 8, even 10 feet tall.

"So what would you think about using the old barn over there? Would that work? Could you create what you need there?"

The barn was old, but it had a certain earthy charm. Angelo could see the possibilities immediately. As fall turned into winter, Angelo, Ben and some friends began fixing up the inside of the barn. Angelo had already converted the horse stalls in the bottom of the barn into his welding area, but the main floor of the barn was a shambles. They began cleaning, putting in insulation and windows, framing doorways, and sheet rocking the walls on the one side. They put in new electric circuits and finished off the floor. In the other half of the street level side, Angelo established his marble cutting and ceramic studio.

This remains a work in progress. We need to figure out a source of heat, get the water connected, and side the barn. Angelo placed several of his large metal sculptures around the entrance to the barn/showroom and randomly in front of Ben's shop. It is eye-catching, attractive and inviting. When the cold central New York weather descends, however, work on the show room has to stop. Then Angelo and Ben return to work building new tables. They also designed and made cherry and oak spice racks, some interesting plant stands, and quilt racks.

Once the showroom is finished, Angelo and Ben will have a "Grand Opening". We will send out notices to friends and family. Our first list of names will be those people who came to Ben's planning party more than 15 years ago. Many of them have kept in contact over the years, but now they can see how far Ben has come. Ben, Angelo and some of their artist friends, will display their work and offer it for sale. They are also working on a website to show their work, explain who they are, and hopefully make some sales.

Angelo posted a short video of Ben and his work on You Tube. Students from Syracuse University, who are studying entrepreneurship for people with disabilities, meet with Ben and Angelo on a weekly basis. Ben's life, his work, is slowly spiraling away from Bob and me. That's what we want. We need to know that Ben can make it with out us. We are not going to be here forever.

Recently, Angelo has begun to talk about retirement. At first I was scared and secretly thought, "Oh, God, here we go again looking for someone to work with Ben." Angelo explained, however, that when he did retire he would still be at Ben's house every day, working in this studio, helping in the show room, making sure all was well for Ben.

"I love that guy." He smiled.

Penny wants to work with Ben again too. She and Ben get along really well, and she loves to work in the shop with him. She spends a lot of time with Ben and has some pretty creative ideas for some new projects. She is skilled and competent.

This makes for a great combination. Plus, Ben now has friends who like to stop at his shop and hang out with him. We are all looking for new opportunities for Ben. A recent development involved three graduate students from Syracuse University who were taking a course in entrepreneurship for people with disabilities. They worked with Ben and Angelo, designing a website, setting up a spread sheet to track inventory and costs, and they created a more efficient floor plan for the shop. Finally, they have helped all of us think of new ways to market Ben's products. Who would have thought?

Chapter 16
YOU NEED TO KICK ME OUT

When Ben spelled out YOU NEED TO KICK ME OUT, I was stunned. It was a blustery winter day and all of us seemed on edge. Grandad had been living with us for almost two years and he and Ben were constantly in a semi state of warfare.

"He scares me. I'm afraid he is going to hurt me." Grandad was sitting in his favorite recliner chair looking out the front windows at the frozen lake. He was talking about Ben, but his was not a new conversation. He had repeatedly said this, often in Ben's presence.

Ben had never hurt him, but his size and race intimidated Grandad. Ben was well over 6 feet now, big and muscular, and it was clear he was Black. Grandad, on the other hand, was small - 5'1", frail, hard of hearing, and 92 years old. He had come to live with us after suffering some strokes at the age of 90. He had been living alone after Bob's mother died several years earlier, but it was evident now that he was not able to take care of himself alone. He deeply resented that he had to live with us. He wanted to stay in his own house but Bob and his two sisters knew that this wasn't possible. None of the family lived nearby and the old neighborhood was changing. Strangers were moving in; fewer people knew him anymore. Even his church was changing; the older people were moving into nursing homes and retirement communities. He just couldn't stay there. He needed daily care and help with routine tasks like bathing, meal preparations, and getting around safely.

Neither of Bob's sisters felt they could manage having him live with them. Their lives were busy and they honestly didn't think they could handle his needs.

"Besides," said Jinie, Bob's younger sister, "you already know how to do this kind of stuff. You've had Ben for a long time."

I think Bob intuitively knew that Grandad would live with us someday. When Bob was still a child, he remembered his grandfather had become ill and Bob's whole family moved in to take care of him.

Bob had received a call from the hospital in Philadelphia. A neighbor had found Grandad and had called the ambulance. The doctor explained that Grandad was being treated, but Bob should get there as soon as possible to make decisions about the next course of action. Bob left with in the hour. He made arrangements for a colleague to cover his classes and drove straight to the hospital, and remained there for several days, until Grandad became more alert and seemed to be recovering. The doctor's told Bob that Grandad would probably stay for a few more days until he was stabilized then, with our permission, he would be transferred into a rehabilitation center so that he could receive the physical therapy he needed. That seemed fine with us. We were not sure what would happen then, but we were relieved that we would have time to think and plan. Bob and I talked on the phone every night. This night he told me what the doctors had said and sounding weary he told me,

"I think I'll visit him in the morning and then drive home for a day or two. I have to see how my students are and I can't expect Bill to cover my classes for ever." The next morning, around 9 AM, Bob called again.

"Get a bed ready. I am bringing him home." He sounded exhausted and frustrated.

"What happened? I thought he was going to stay there. I thought..." Bob cut me off.

"The doctor is releasing him in a few hours. I am going to his house to get some clothes packed and to close up the place for now. Get a bed ready. I'll see you tonight sometime. I love you."

My heart broke for Bob. His father had never been one of his favorite people. He simply wasn't a very likable person. I felt waves of anger rush over me. Grandad had been the one who said that Ben wasn't welcome in his house, and now we were supposed to welcome Grandad here, in our house. There was no time to get stuck on these thoughts, however, we had to get ready for him. Sherry, our oldest daughter was living with us then while she decided on graduate school. She and I drafted a quick plan to convert our downstairs study into a makeshift bedroom. It was next to the bathroom, which was good. We emptied all the furniture into the living room and carried a bed frame, mattress and box springs from upstairs. We covered the doorway with a double bed sheet thinking that would give him some temporary privacy. We scrubbed, cleaned, got towels and bed linens ready. By the time Bob and Grandad arrived, the room was ready and Sherry and I were totally exhausted. Bob looked pale and drawn and Grandad looked vacant and confused. He kept protesting,

"Bob, I want to go home. Take me home. I don't want to be here. Take me home." His voice was feeble and weak, but his intent was clear.

We tried to reassure him that he was going to be fine, but he resisted everything we did. "Put me away then. Let me die. Let me die, Bob. I don't want to be here."

He refused to eat. Bob knew that Grandad was exhausted from the 5-hour drive, so he didn't push.

"Here, Dad, this will be your bed. Let's get your pajamas on and you can rest."

Beautiful Ben

"I don't care what happens to me. I want to die. Leave me alone. Let me die."
He looked at me.

"Tell her to go away. I don't want her here. Leave me alone." He made some
feeble attempts to push Bob's hands away as he tried to unbutton Grandad's shirt.
I backed out of the room quietly while Bob gently got him ready for bed. Always the
optimist, I thought things would get better. Sherry, Ben and I looked at each other,
unsure of what to do.

"How about a glass of wine, Mom." Sherry went into the kitchen.

"Let's see how he is in the morning. Maybe after a good nights sleep he will feel
better." It was all I could think to say. I was so wrong. It never got better. Grandad
was miserable and sour for the entire four years he lived with us before he died
at the age of 94. He was angry with Bob for taking him away from his home. He
thought I was lazy and didn't know how to cook because he didn't like the food I
made. He was scared of Ben. Sherry and Penny seemed to be the only people he
would respond to, although he often didn't seem to recognize them.

Near the end of his life, Penny took a leave from her work to care for him. Every
day he would ask her who she was.

"I'm Penny, your grand daughter."

"No you're not. You're not my grand daughter." He would protest.

One day Penny asked him to tell her about his grand daughter. She wanted to
know what he was thinking, and why he denied who she was.

"Oh, Penny is a little girl. Your too big to be her." Penny laughed out loud, and
then she got down on her hands and knees with her face next to his knee. He was
sitting in his wheelchair.

"Hi Grandad. It's me, Penny, your grand daughter." She smiled sweetly up at
him.

"Penny, Penny." He smiled with recognition. Penny chuckled.

Having Grandad live with us was difficult. When his health had improved we
tried to get him interested in the kind of activities he had enjoyed before. We offered
to take him to church, but he refused. We suggested going to the local senior center
to meet other people.

"I won't go and you can't make me." was his reply. He would fold his arms on
his chest, close his eyes and refuse to speak. We took him for rides but he wouldn't
look out the windows. Once we were sure that he was not going to live with either
of Bob's sisters, we suggested that he might be happier in a retirement community

where there were other people his age. "NO!" We took him to see a local complex just so he could see how nice it was. When we drove in the entranceway, he closed his eyes. He wasn't sleeping. He was just being arrogant.

Most disturbing, however, was his attitude toward Ben. Bob and I often remarked privately to each other that we felt like referees. Grandad would make some impolite or down right nasty comment and Ben would retaliate by walking close to him, hovering, intimidating him.

"Okay, I've got Ben, you get Grandad." We tried to keep them separate just to preserve the peace. Sometimes, over the years, people have asked, "why does he do that? Or "what does he mean?" as they tried to understand Ben's actions and speech. Not Grandad. He never asked anything about Ben. He rarely spoke to him, but often about him.

"I don't know why you keep him." That was the one statement that always riled me, but I bit my tongue.

"If I had to make the choice between the two of you, hmmm..." I would think to myself.

Why did Ben want to move out?

When Ben said that we needed to kick him out, and later elaborated that he wanted to move out, I jumped to the conclusion that he had finally had it with Grandad and wanted to escape. There were many times when I felt the same way. Why shouldn't he? But that wasn't what Ben was thinking, although the tension in the house may have precipitated his thinking. It never occurred to me to ask why Ben wanted to move out. There certainly had been times when his behavior had made this idea look pretty good. Of course we would never really kick him out, but Bob and I had frequently talked about what might eventually happen. We had always thought that Ben would live someplace else when he was an adult. We were not prepared to think about this now. Ben was only 18 and still in high school. It had not occurred to us that Ben might have a different agenda. One lesson we learned from his using facilitated communication, however, was not to make assumptions. Years later, we did ask.

"Ben when and why did you decide that you wanted to move out?"

TRY TO LIVE ON MY OWN LIKE A MAN AND I WAS READY TO LIVE ON MY OWN JUST LIKE MY TWO SISTERS.

"Well, we have always planned on that. Let's think about what that might look like." Bob and I had known from the beginning that we didn't want Ben to live in

Beautiful Ben

an institution. When he was still quite young we had specified in our wills that we did not want anyone to place Ben in an institution. We had even constructed a collection of people, our "chosen family" we had called them, who were named in our wills who promised us that they would make sure Ben would not go to an institution if and when we died. Now that he was older, 18 at the time of this conversation, institutions were closing, but group homes and "supported residential units" were viewed as positive alternatives, but not to us. We had spent a lot of our personal and professional time advocating for the closure of our local institution. Bob served on the governing board of directors for over 20 years, and he never wavered in his belief that, with the right supports, people with complex disabilities could live successfully in local neighborhoods. By the time Ben was 18, we had become friends with a number of individuals with disabilities, some who had lived in institutions for years. We listened to their stories. It was apparent; they had never been given a choice. We wanted Ben to have a choice and a voice in his future.

Bob was also on the board of a local human service agency, Onondaga Community Living, that provided residential and vocational supports for adults with disabilities. It was a small agency with a mission statement that clearly articulated "listening, focusing, helping, supporting, exploring and developing...for the individual..." (2001. Fratangelo, Olney & Lehr. p. 86). The executive director, Pat Fratangelo, had been one of Bob's students in the mid 1970's. He liked her and respected her values regarding people with disabilities, even the most challenging ones, which was the main reason he had agreed to go on the board. He had previously worked with her when she was the Residential Coordinator of a local ARC. He had been on that board too.

Bob had told Pat that he doubted that Onondaga Community Living could ever serve Ben. Over the years, however, Bob had told Pat about Ben. When Ben indicated that he wanted to move out of our house, Bob mentioned it to Pat. She asked him if we were aware of a new approach to planning, called Person Centered Planning. We had read about this and had even heard some presentations concerning it at the annual TASH (an international disability rights organization) conferences. It seemed like a good idea and we thought it might help us sort out with Ben what were the best alternatives.

We didn't do anything immediately. We were still struggling with Grandad and I was trying to write my dissertation. Poor man, he had never seen computers, so when I spent hours typing on mine, he complained to Bob that all I ever did was watch television. I had to laugh, but it also stung just a little. Grandad died in the summer of

1994, sitting in his favorite chair with the sun shining on him. Penny and I had been with him all day and he just quietly went to sleep. He had finally gotten his wish.

Ben's Planning Party

After his funeral we began in earnest to explore Ben's idea. It didn't take us long to decide to host a "Planning Party" for Ben. By this time we had read a lot about what we should do and Pat had suggested a friend who was experienced at leading these kinds of discussions. We picked a date and began to make a list of people to invite. Ben seemed quite pleased with the attention and focus. Eventually we invited friends who knew each of us, but mostly people who really cared about Ben or knew the system well and could ultimately advise us.

January 10, 1994

Dear Friends,

We are beginning a process of planning for Ben's transition out of school and into a new future. Since you have been involved in our family's life, we would like to invite you to be part of this process.

On January 29th, a Saturday, we will be getting together at our house beginning at 10:30 AM and ending sometime in the late afternoon. We will provide lunch and lots of coffee and munchies. All you need to bring are your ideas and your interest in offering your insights.

A friend of ours will help us as a group go through a process of identifying ways we can help and support Ben and the decisions he wants to make about his future. We really hope that you can be part of this process! Even if you can only come for part of the time we really need your help and input.

Please give one of us a call to let us know whether you can join us. As you can imagine, we are excited about helping Ben plan his own future, and we are also a bit scared. Your support is very important to all of us.

Fourteen people arrived the morning of the party. It was a bitter cold, very snowy day. Our ten-foot long supper table was covered with bagels, cream cheese, donuts, breads, coffee and teas. Later we would clear this off and serve homemade hot soup, chili, salads, and breads. Food has always been an important focus for our family so it seemed appropriate that we should have plenty available for everyone.

Bob began the morning by thanking everyone for coming. Then he explained that Cheryl, the facilitator, was not able to get here because of the bad weather. As a family we had decided to move ahead on our own because the planning party was

Beautiful Ben

very important to Ben and us. Sherry had agreed to step in as the group discussion leader. She had taped large sheets of newsprint on the walls of our living room and was poised with markers in each hand, ready to go.

"We need your help." I knew it was hard for Bob to say this.

"It has been difficult if not totally impossible for us to ask for help in the past, but many people have stepped in and helped us. Now we realize that in order for Ben to make it successfully in his future and, in order for him to make good decisions about where he will live, work, play and feel good, we need our friends to help us." Bob took a deep breath. Everyone was waiting.

Sherry took over and explained that, through this process, we hoped people would get to know Ben better and ultimately help us determine what the next steps should be. She set about explaining the plan as follows: We would,

1. Discuss Ben's routines now and what he could add to enable him to be more independent and live in his own place.
2. Discuss Ben's interests and what else he might enjoy so that his work and free time would be productive and enjoyable.
3. Discuss what goals Ben might want to set for himself and what would be needed for him to accomplish these.

She gave everyone a 10-minute break to think about these and when we reconvened she led us through a vibrant and productive discussion. Bob and I sat in the middle of everyone and Ben sat off to the edge with a friend. When discussing Ben's routines and his difficulty with sleeping at night, he typed out JITTERY, UPSET, ABOUT BEING OUT OF CONTROL. This was a theme that he would return to periodically.

By the end of the day we knew the following things about Ben:

Things he dislikes-
- Not having enough dish soap, plastic bottles or water to play with
- Getting dirty or slimy
- Losing control
- Walking down hills in rough or uneven terrain
- Being controlled or restrained and/or told what to do (as a command)
- Not having enough money
- Things he finds boring-
- High school
- Long lectures on boring topics

Things that frustrate Ben-
- Being treated like a child

- Not having money
- Not being able to control himself
- Seeing others not trying to control themselves
- Being independent

Things that Ben finds scary-
- Being out of control
- Climbing trees
- Old thoughts
- Old bad memories
- Grandad going to Loretto (a nursing home)
- Dying
- Looking stupid
- Syracuse Developmental Center - the local institution
- Large black men (reminders of being abused)
- Not knowing where people are (people he cares about)
- Not knowing when people are coming back

These themes have repeated themselves over the years. Some have changed, but basically, this is truly a reflection of who Ben was and is today. In conclusion, the group identified the following themes that remain salient today:
- Ben worried about losing control of himself
- He liked to be with friends, especially people his own age
- He liked to make his own choices
- Ben liked to organize his work himself
- He had ways of calming himself down
- He was learning ways of controlling his body when working with tools
- He wanted to continue to work in the local library

As to his future, Ben wanted to live in his own house. He wanted to work but he was not sure doing what just yet. He had some ideas, but mostly he wanted to have friends. He believed they would be there and could help him. We had come to a natural end. It was past four o'clock and we were tired but felt good about what had transpired. Later Ben would type the following letter to those who attended.

THANK YOU FOR COM,INGT TO MY PARTY. FEEL GREAT
BECAUSE YOU HELPEWD MY WAY UP OUT OF THE
TERRIBLE DREADFUL AUTIESM. BEN.

Beautiful Ben

The party was over, and now the work began.

Our first question for Ben was where to live if he wasn't going to continue to live with us. Bob and I had assumed that Ben would eventually live next door to us or down the street so that we could oversee what was happening. We had already discussed renting or possibly buying a neighbor's house two doors away. She was getting older and she and her husband were considering moving to Florida. It seemed ideal to us. Ben had different ideas. He revealed these slowly through his typing, but he was clear.

When asked, Ben typed the following.

"Where do you want to live?"

SYRACXUS

"Do you have any idea where in Syracuse?"

IN THE UNIVERSITY AREA

"What kind of place do you want to live in?"

HOUDS E

He didn't want to live down the street from us. He wanted to live near where he had gone to high school. He was familiar with this area and knew many people who lived there. He also informed us that he certainly did not want to live in an apartment. He had visited Sherry and Christian, her new husband, where they lived in Washington, DC in an apartment.

CAME TOGETHER WHEN SHERRY MOVED WITH CHRISTIAN
TO WASHINGTON. NOT WANT NEW APARTMENT BECAUSE
GREAT NEED FOR PEACE AND QUIET.

This certainly made sense. Ben had lived in a house his whole life. In subsequent discussions, Ben also recognized that if his behavior resulted in breaking or destroying his home, things that had happened in the past, he knew he would be "kicked out." He didn't want this to happen. He believed he could live more responsibly if he were in his own house. Hmmm ...could he?

Over the years Ben had done some pretty damaging things to our house. He had smashed his head through windows, used a sharp knife to gouge our supper table and doorjambs. He had cut electric wires. He had pulled the insulation out of ceilings and walls. What would he do in his own house? When we asked him he simply said he wanted his own bedroom and a space large enough for a shop to do some building projects.

Were we crazy in thinking this could happen for Ben? We had no idea, but we moved ahead. A close friend recommended a good real estate agent and we arranged to meet with him. Bob and I envisioned that Ben could live in a duplex; he and a roommate could be on one side and support staff would live on the other. Once again, Ben had his own ideas. He communicated that he wanted to live alone. ALONE!

What? I couldn't believe my eyes/ears (he was typing). I took a breath and tried to think of what Ben really wanted.

"So Ben, let's think about this a bit more. We have time to plan, so let's do that." My heart was racing and I was thinking fast. I didn't want to lose him, to make him think we didn't trust and respect that he could make it. I also knew living alone was not going to be an option.

"Hmmm. Living alone. Well, that's a pretty big step. You have lived with us for so long. Living alone would be very different." My mind was churning with what could happen. I didn't want to discourage him, but I also knew I had to be honest.

"So, how about if we make a list of the times when you need support to do something. You know, like doing your laundry or cooking a meal. We could also write down the things you can do on your own, like showering or brushing your teeth or using the microwave if the right food is available. Then we could work on your learning how to do those things that you needed. What do you think of that plan? Oh yea, in the meantime, we can begin to look for houses. What do you think?"

THINK YES.

So that is how it all began. We posted lists on the refrigerator and every time someone helped Ben do something we would write it on the sheet that said "With Support", but if Ben could do something on his own, it was posted on the list "By My Self." It was really a good way of determining where he was. We also began to introduce the idea of loneliness and being alone.

"So Ben, I was wondering if you have thought about being lonely? You are used to living in our house that is so full of people and activity. Living alone might be hard." I wanted to say more, but I let it go at that. I knew he would think about it and he did.

The house hunt begins

In the meantime, Ben and I began looking at prospective houses. This actually proved to be quite a funny experience. Usually the seller's realtor was at the house, prepared to make a great sales pitch about why this house was "just what you must be looking for..." but when I explained that Ben was going to be making the decision and also would be the person living in the house, the reactions were - well, shall we say - very mixed. I often wondered what each one was reacting to; Ben in general, his blackness, his youth, his white mother, his inability to speak coherently, his autism, - who knows. Ben and I looked at over two dozen houses in the general university neighborhood. Invariably, we would enter a house and Ben would make a bee line for the frig, open the door, check out the contents, and then turn and look at me as if, "Okay, let's check the rest of this place out." Sometimes, after checking out the frig, he would simply walk out the front door. Generally, however, he liked every house he saw. I often saw things that made me dislike the house; repairs that were needed, not located near a bus line, or too expensive. Over time Ben became more discerning too.

All the while, Bob and I were trying to figure out how we could finance all of this. Since we were just about to pay off the final mortgage payment on our own house, we considered refinancing our home to get the money for the down payment on Ben's. We began to contact banks about the best rates, and we contacted our attorney to see about Ben becoming the homeowner. Time was going bye and Ben and I were becoming a bit discouraged. We just couldn't find the right house.

"Maybe this is a bad idea." I said to Bob one night. I didn't want Ben to think I was going to back out, but I was getting tired. I was also beginning to think that maybe Ben had changed his mind. Maybe he really wanted to stay living with us. I had mixed feelings.

"What does Ben want?" Bob asked. Of course, that was the right question. It had not occurred to me that Ben also might be getting discouraged.

"So Ben, what do you think about all of this? Should we keep looking? Is this what you want to do, look for the right house?"

HOUSE, YES. I knew that Ben would often repeat what ever he heard last, so I changed the question, just to be sure.

"Ben, this is important. We have been looking for a house for quite some time. I just want to be sure we are doing the right thing. You know, that we are on the right track. What do you think?" I expected him to repeat "right thing" or "right track", but instead he said HOUSE LOOK YES. I knew we had to keep going.

The interest rates were plummeting and I was getting anxious that we find something before they started rising again. By chance Doc, Ben's former teacher, knew of a house that was going up for sale soon. It was close to his house. In fact he and his wife were interested in looking at it themselves. We decided to look at it together. Ben liked it instantly and so did I. Although it was an older home it had recently been repaired; the price was reasonable; it was in a great location, there was even a little grocery down the block. We looked at it several times before making an offer.

After some negotiating, our purchase offer was accepted and we applied for a mortgage. An ironic note was that we ended up using our inheritance from Grandad to make the initial down payment.

"I'll bet Grandad is turning over in his grave." Bob said with a wry smile on his face. I had to chuckle too. It was truly ironic and I loved it.

It was a big house within several blocks of Syracuse University and Jowonio School. Ed Smith Elementary School was less than two blocks away and the junior high and high school that Ben had attended were within walking distance. There was a lovely porch that extended across the front of the house. A cherry tree was in the front yard and, over the years, this was a favorite place for Ben to climb. Often he frightened unsuspecting people who were walking underneath, but the neighbors knew him and enjoyed seeing him climb.

There was a large living room and dining room, a small entrance foyer with stairs leading up, and a miniscule kitchen with a tiny breakfast nook, a screened in back porch, a decent back yard and a two car garage. The attic had been finished off into a separate apartment with a half bath. Ben's bedroom overlooked the back yard. The biggest draw back to the house was that it only had one full bathroom and that was on the second floor. Ben loves to take long, I mean really, really long baths, so this solitary bathroom posed problems especially when women were there. They seemed to manage most of the time. Ben also likes to use other peoples' shampoo, which posed some tensions until everyone agreed to keep their shampoo in their bedrooms or in locked cabinets. Ben knew these bottles belonged to others, but when he wanted a bubble bath, the lure as too great.

We have the house, now what about the supports?

Once he knew that we were going to buy this house, the "Lancaster House" Ben called it, he was so ready to get moved. It was really quite funny, but also scary. Bob and I knew that the easy part was over. Now the hard part really began - finding live-in support for Ben and worse, letting him go. We had no idea how to go about this, but we assumed that because Ben had been in inclusive classrooms through out his school career, there would be people who knew him and might want to live with him. We were totally wrong. Most of Ben's friends from school had gone off to college, joined the Army, or simply moved away.

Ben said, "ROOMMATES SHOULD BE NICE AND UNDERSTANDING." I couldn't agree more, but how would we find them? We made up fliers and sent these to friends. We talked to everyone we knew who would listen. We went back to the people who had attended Ben's planning party. We tried to spread the word far and wide, but nothing happened. In a way, although I refused to admit it to myself, I think I was relieved.

I really wasn't prepared for Ben to move out, to be on his own. I kept thinking of all the support we provided. We did that because he needed it and we loved him. Or was I just fooling myself. Was I trying to make a case for not letting him go? Was this really about Ben and what he wanted, or was it about me and what I was afraid of? Was I being over-protective? When I finally acknowledged these feelings to myself I began thinking of everything we had worked for. Bob and I wanted each of our children to be independent and happy; to have a life as each of them wanted to live it. Although I had been ready when Sherry went off to college, I was really scared later when she wanted to travel to Morocco, Europe and China. When she decided to move to Germany, the first time, I felt I had lost her. In a way, I had, but that was part of growing up. When Penny tried college, I knew even before she left that it was a mistake. I knew she would be back, but I wasn't prepared for her independence. She was ready to grow up in her own way. She has always been a free spirit who has pushed our limits, and leaving home was no exception. College was not her thing. She planned to live her life on her own terms and she did. I wasn't always happy with the decisions that Sherry and Penny made for themselves, but I had confidence that they could manage. For Ben, however, things were just moving too fast. Or was it too fast for me?

It took me a while to really think this through and to realize this wasn't about me, it was about Ben and his need to express his independence. I thought about all the families I had met over the years whose son or daughter with a disability still lived with them. I vowed that we were not going to be like them. I didn't want to see us tottering along in our old age, holding Ben's hand (literally and figuratively), keeping him a child forever, because we didn't know how to let him go. I didn't want my life to become so dependent upon Ben's need for my support that I couldn't let go. I needed to know that he could make it without me. My parents had died young, I might too, then what would happen to him? I finally realized that I wanted to see Ben living his own life, feeling free, being an adult, having friends. Yes, I knew there were going to be risks. I had to accept that.

Ben wanted us to put an ad in the local newspaper under the "Room Mates Wanted" column.

"How did he know about this option?" I wondered. My first thought was that no one would answer the ad. Then what would we do? We talked about it and finally decided to try it. Nothing else seemed to be working so there seemed little to lose. Ben wrote the first part of the ad.

HOUSE MATES/COMPANIONS WANTED: YOUNG MAN WITH AUTISM MOVING INTO UNIVERSITY AREA LOOKING FOR HOUSE MATES/ COMPANIONS. SUBSIDIZED RENT MAY BE POSSIBLE. FOR MORE INFORMATION CALL SUE AT - and our home phone number was included. When he typed "with autism" I had mixed feelings. On the one hand I thought it was courageous of him to be so forthright, but on the other I was afraid that no one would answer the ad. I began rehearsing what I would say to him when no one called. In the meantime, Bob and I figured that if we could find even one person who wanted to try it, we could reduce their rent in return for supporting him. Ben would pay the monthly mortgage payment from his Social Security check. If we could find additional roommates, their rent would cover the rest of the mortgage payment and utilities. It seemed like a plan, IF, and it was a huge IF we could find the roommates.

In preparing the ad, Ben had coached me about what he wanted and did not want in a roommate so that when people called I could do some initial screening for him. The following criteria were important to Ben:

1. People generally the same age.
2. No females. They tended to mother him too much, and he had lived with two sisters.
3. People who would not see him as odd or a freak.

Much to my surprise, five people responded to the ad. I would introduce myself as Ben's mother and explain that, because of his autism, he was not able to talk on the phone. If they were still interested I asked if they had ever had experience with someone with autism. None of them knew anything about autism. Generally, they wanted to know what they would have to do to qualify for the subsidized rent. They all sounded nice, but it is so hard to tell over the phone.

"What was I looking for?" I kept thinking. How could I tell just from a few brief moments on the phone, whom Ben would be safe with? By nature, I am a very trusting person, but wasn't this going too far? I had so many thoughts and questions. Then one young man impressed me in a different way.

Beautiful Ben

Chapter 17

Ben moves out

"I don't know anything about autism. I really don't. I've heard of it, and I am sure I could learn. To be honest, however, I need to find a place of my own because I live with my mother right now, and I have to move." Before I could say much else he continued.

"How about if your son and I meet each other first, you know, before we get too far. If he doesn't like me or I think I can't do it, then that's it. What do you think?"

I could tell he was as nervous as I was. Neither of us had any idea what we were doing. My mind was racing.

"He sounds good, logical, rational, and what? Nice. Is 'nice' good enough? He lived with his mother; that sounded good, and his first interest was in meeting Ben, not talking about autism. I told him I would have to talk it over with Ben and call him back. I told Ben what this young man, Darrell, had said and asked if he wanted to meet him.

"WANT TO MEET HIM? YES."

We arranged to meet on the weekend.

Darrell phoned again the next day. I thought he was calling to back out, that he had changed his mind, that he had found another place to live, but I was wrong. He told me that he was still eager to meet Ben, but he had another question.

"I have a friend who also needs to find a new place to live. I was wondering if you might be interested in having two people live with Ben? If you are, I can bring him with me."

A few days later Ben, Darrell, Jesse and I met. It was early summer and quite hot so we sat out on our back porch. I had no idea of what to say or do, so I decided to take my lead from Ben. We all introduced ourselves and I explained that I was only here to assist Ben with his communication. I sat back and watched. Both young men were the same age as Ben, (20). Both were very good-looking, well dressed, and extremely polite. They talked directly to Ben and seemed fascinated with him. Likewise, Ben seemed happy and calm. Something was happening and it seemed to be good. They never really asked much about the autism or what that meant for Ben, they just talked. At one point, the three of them invited me to leave "you know, not to be rude, but to see if we want to make this work." I went into the house, but I truly wanted to listen in, but I didn't. They sat out there for a long time. I heard laughing, and that made me smile. When I went back outside, Darrell said,

"Well, we decided to try it, right Ben?" He looked at Ben and smiled and Ben smiled back. Jesse smiled too and nodded his head in agreement. It was a beginning.

Later Darrell explained why he had answered the ad.

"I was bored at home. I had registered at a temp agency. I was watching the ads. I saw this. I was struck with the idea of it. The whole thing. I liked the idea of being a companion, a friend. I saw it as a good way to both go to school and not have to work a real job. It seemed like a job that would not require much. I could devote myself to school. I called and left a message on your answering machine. I didn't think anything would happen. It was a private home, and I didn't think they would call me back. But you did. I talked with you and I enjoyed it. I had just reconnected with Jesse, an old friend, and we talked about this living arrangement as a possibility. I like to be with people and I saw this as a possibility to get something by learning, and I thought I could get a lot out of giving something back. I figured we would both be growing."

Jesse said,

"At first, it was the promise of money and a place to live but once I committed to it I wasn't going to give up."

Moving in

Darrell and Jesse were prepared to move in a few weeks later. It was early August. Bob and I intended that once they were settled, Ben could begin to visit for brief periods of time so that they all could be come acquainted. We thought over about a 6-month period, Ben's visits could get longer and eventually they all would be ready for Ben to move in permanently. Ben had very different ideas. They moved in and two days later so did Ben.

We had spent the previous two days packing and getting Ben ready. He was quite excited and happy. Bob and I kept asking ourselves, "Do we have any idea what we are doing?" Invariably the answer was NO! We didn't really know anything about these two young men. We didn't ask for references, nor did we do a background check. We trusted them, but even more we trusted Ben's reaction to them. Over the years we have realized that Ben has wonderful "Bull Shit" radar. He senses out people who are genuine. We can see it in the way he interacts with people. If he touches them or holds onto their arm or puts his arm around their shoulder he trusts this person. His response to others, for reasons that we cannot always fathom, is to walk away or completely ignore the person. If he feels that a person is demeaning him or treating him like an autistic person, he will become agitated and begin to lose some control. Darrell and Jesse treated Ben like a friend, a peer.

The first few days were chaotic. Just getting the house arranged was a challenge. Bob and I raided our attic for furniture and kitchenware. Fortunately, we had accumulated lots of junk from Grandad's house and there were left over items from other people who had moved in and out of our house over the years. Darrell brought some of his own possessions, but Jesse just had a rolled up piece of foam rubber, a blanket and pillow, and a brown paper bag with his clothes in it.

Ben described the first few days. VERY CRAZY. DRIVING EACH OTHER CRAZY. DARRELL SAID ZANY THINKS, FUNNY THINGS. MUCH BETTER JUST KNOWING MY FRIENDS HAD GREAT FEELINGS FOR ME.

It took a while to get adjusted to each other, but eventually some sort of crazy routine was established. We continued to look for additional housemates to help pay the expenses. A high school friend of Darrell and Jesse's tried living there, but it just wasn't a good match. He was pretty immature at first and Darrell felt he was not treating Ben with respect. I talked to him and tried to explain what we expected, but he just wasn't ready for this kind of responsibility. It was his first time living away from home and he wanted to have his girl friend over all the time. Ben didn't like this. Finally, we all agreed it was time for him to move out.

Over time there were many different people who lived at the Lancaster house, each usually for about a year. There was a wonderful Canadian graduate student who was studying classical music. He enjoyed Ben and found him fascinating. He liked to teach Ben how to draw on the computer. Together they would listen to music. There was another young man, a foreign student from Sri Lanka. He also found Ben fascinating and liked the way Ben accepted him as a friend. There was a fellow who had just returned from the Peace Corps and was trying to decide what to do with his life. Darrell's girl friend moved in, but when she graduated a few months later, she and Darrell announced that they were going to move out west. She had accepted a job and they planned to get married the following year. It had been a good year for Ben, and it was hard for him to see Darrell leave. They had become good friends. Jesse said he wanted to stay and Ben agreed. It was over 10 years later that Jesse finally left also, but that is another story.

Agency Support

As we were engaging in this complicated process, Bob and I realized we needed to ask for help again. Hard as it was, we knew we needed better and more consistent supports for Ben. Jesse was moving from job to job and people who moved into the Lancaster house often found Jesse hard to live with. They got along fine with Ben, generally, but there was always a tension between Jesse and others. He was very protective of Ben and this posed some problems too. We thought we could deal with this, but what we really needed was both financial and programmatic support to keep all of this in place.

Bob was still on the Board of Directors for Onondaga Community Living so he approached Pat, the executive director, asking her to give us some advice. We still, at that point, had not considered that Ben would be eligible for services from her agency. I am not sure why, but I guess we thought he was too tough and would need too much, plus Bob didn't want to impose on his friendship with Pat. We just didn't think it through. We thought we would have to do everything ourselves. Pat listened and said she would see what she could do.

Medicaid Waiver

Pat told us that New York State Office of Mental Retardation and Developmental Disabilities was applying to the federal government for the Medicaid Waiver. We had heard about this, but we didn't understand the implications for Ben. Pat briefly explained that states had the option to request Medicaid monies to pay for services for people like Ben. Historically, these monies had been used to fund the operational costs of large-scale institutions, but as deinstitutionalization occurred, and as more and more states could demonstrate how they could support the same individuals for less money in the community, more states were opting to apply for this funding source. It sounded promising, but Pat cautioned us that it would not be an easy process to access the money.

"It's a pretty long and complicated application process." Pat explained. "Basically, there are two levels of approval, one at the local level and one at the state level. If we can keep Ben's total costs below the local level cap for funding we may stand a better chance, but there are no guarantees." Bob had to chuckle. For years he had been asking the director of the local institution to give us the same amount of money he would receive if Ben lived in his institution.

"I'll even settle for half." He would joke.

What Pat was talking about now was even less than that, but we thought it was worth the try. She asked what specifically Ben wanted and needed; what we wanted. She didn't ask us to figure out how to fit that into the application, or how to translate his needs into habilitation or residential goals.

She simply asked, "Ben what do you need? What do you want?" Then she worked on creating a Medicaid Waiver Plan for Ben. We were confident that Pat would not try to fit Ben into some sort of model program. Nor would she force him to select services that would not benefit him, but could be funded.

One of our primary concerns was to be reassured that Ben's house would not become a "residential site" or a "certified home" by state standards. We wanted Ben and Jesse, and their other housemates to recognize that this was their home. It didn't belong to the state and would not be run by some outside providers. They could live there as friends, Ben's friends, not his staff. We didn't want the housemates to have to participate in unnecessary training or have to keep logs and journals of how Ben spent his time, when he had problems, or what goals they were working on with him. Of course, we understood the need for legal compliance issues and safety needs, but we didn't want anyone to lose sight of the fact that this was Ben's home, his life.

Pat listened to us and began to work out a plan. She attached costs to each service that would be needed and she figured out a budget based on these. Ever mindful of the local level cap, she struggled to keep within that limit. Finally the application was ready to go. Pat took it to the local Disability Service Organization personally and explained each item with the budget people and anyone else who needed to understand what we were trying to do. She never bothered us with the details, she just did what she believed was right for Ben because it was what he and we said was needed and wanted. Ben's application was approved and life went on.

....

A story – Ben's decisions

In preparing for a public presentation about his home and living with friends he was asked the following questions. His answers are here too.

Question: Ben, you, Darrel and Jesse seem to have good relationships with each other. What makes it work?

Answer: WE TAKE CARE OF EACH OTHER.

Question: What would you tell parents of children with disabilities about how to help them meet people, have friendships, and be more on their own?

Answer: HAVE JUST KIDS BE TOGETHER.

Question: Do you mean parents should arrange for kids to spend time together?

Answer: YES.

Question: Some parents worry that their child is an imposition on others, or that some people would not want to be with their child because of the disability. What would you say to those parents?

Answer: STOP THINKING YOUR KIDS WASTE OTHER PEOPLES FEELINGS AND ESTABLISH KIDS WISHES.

Question: What do you mean, "establish kids wishes"?

Answer: ASK KIDS WHAT THEY WANT.

Question: What do you think kids want?

Answer: TO BE LIKED.

Question: Does the disability get in the way of liking kids?

Answer: GET FRIENDS WITH PEOPLE OTEHR THAN DISABLED FRIENDS.

Here is what Jesse said:

Question: You and Ben spend a lot of time together in public places. Undoubtedly, there have been awkward moments when Ben was created problems. What makes you stick with him? Why are you willing to take new risks with him?

Answer: I don't see Ben differently, only the situation differently. If people give us dirty looks, I just ignore them. I think they are ignorant people. Ben and I are friends now. I feel like we have a brotherly relationship. What I like about Ben is he lets me be me. I don't have to pretend I am anyone else. I never get bored. I don't have to play a role. Ben accepts me for who I am. There have been adventures like not knowing where he is or whose shower he is in. I have had to figure out what to do when he has headaches and/or sleepless nights. I have learned how to maintain a sense of humor. I have no time to be bored. We are friends.

. . . .

What happened when there were problems?

Problems were bound to arise. We knew that. At first, however, we were not sure how to handle these, but we did agree to keep talking with each other, problem solving, and supporting each other through whatever decisions and solutions were made. We also told Darrel and Jesse they could call us any time day or night if they needed help.

One of the major problems Jesse, Ben and Darrell had to deal with early on was Ben's compulsion to leave the house in the middle of the night when everyone else was sleeping. Because he often left without waking anyone, and because several times his forays ended him in trouble with the police getting involved, we needed to figure out ways to help Ben stay safe. Collectively, we decided that there should be an alarm system in the house which would activate once it was armed when anyone opened the door or window.

. . . .

A story – Broken Windows

"Hey Sue, we have a problem." It was Jesse on the phone.

"Ben's okay." He knew to say this right away so that I would not be afraid.

"I don't know when he did it, but he must have left during the night and he had a hammer. He smashed the windows in the house across the street. The landlady is really, and I mean really, pissed! She wants him arrested. I tried to explain about Ben, but she is furious. I think I convinced her to talk to you first." I left moments later.

Describing the landlady as pissed was putting it mildly.

"People like him should be locked up!" She shouted at me. I had gone across the street and introduced myself as Ben's mother. I could see the instant shock in her eyes, and then the unspoken accusation - "Who did you sleep with?"

"I am truly sorry for what happened. I will have your windows repaired as quickly as possible. Ben has autism. I don't know why he did this." I was speaking rapidly, but my words were not helping.

"My tenant was terrified. He thought he was going to die! He thought he was going to be murdered!" She screamed at me.

"I was thinking of moving back here myself, but I can't do that now that I know a wacko lives so close."

All I could do was stand there and let her vent. Finally, when it seemed she had exhausted all her venom, I repeated that Ben had not hurt anyone. Yes, he had smashed her windows and I didn't know why, but he was not a wacko or a danger. I tried to keep my voice calm and reassuring, but my heart was pounding and I could feel the tears welling in my eyes.

"If you will let me, I will clean up all the broken glass right now. And I'll call a repair person immediately to see how quickly we can get the repairs done." I knew my voice sounded like I was pleading. Well, I guess I was. She agreed so I quickly got a dustpan and brush and picked up every shard of glass I could find. My thoughts were all over the place. I looked at the broken windows and suddenly realized the enormity of it all.

"Oh shit! Wouldn't you know he would pick beveled glass windows to break? This is going to cost me a fortune." I was crestfallen, but I kept my mouth shut and quietly cleaned.

Obviously, she had not exhausted her frustration and fear. All the while I was on my hands and knees cleaning up her floor, she continued to protest that a "person like him" should not be out in the community unattended. I thought about telling her that Ben had lived across the street from her for over a year and nothing had happened until now, but I let it go. I just wanted to be done and leave. I was hurt, angry and then totally dumbfounded when she told me she was a high school teacher.

"These kids, you know, the ones they want to include in my classes, have no right to be there. They can't learn. They should be put away and kept there."

It was all I could do to not bite her ankles as I finished cleaning her floor.

Beautiful Ben

Why did Ben do this? Who knows. He couldn't explain it. It was just a compulsion to which he had succumbed. Was this the end of it? No.

I had the windows repaired. She sold the house. I was glad. Ben was never able to tell us what had happened, what he was thinking, or why he felt compelled to engage in such actions. And then, it sort of happened again, but this time, the outcome was different. Again, he left the house and went into a house down the street. An older Asian couple owned it. The wife had been scared but later she said that she recognized Ben. She knew he did not mean to hurt her. She called her husband from the other room. He told Ben to leave.

"Go home. Go home." He said. Ben left and went home. No accusations of "wacko" behavior. No police calls. Just neighbors who seemed to understand that Ben was different. After that, they locked their doors. Jesse told us about this incident long after it happened.

Another story – Now it's a knife

Darrell told of another time. "Last night while everyone was asleep Ben woke up, went downstairs and left the house. He left by way of the window either in the dining room or the kitchen. They were both left open. The police report described that "at approximately 4am, banging on the front door by four police officers woke me up. Opening the front door I saw Ben sitting on the floor of our front porch with the officers standing all around him. As soon as Ben saw me he got up, came in and ran up the stairs. I invited the police into the house. They began to tell me about the incidents that had transpired not too long prior to their arrival at the house. Ben was at the store, the little market down the street with a knife. He was using the knife to try and cut the lock. Someone saw Ben and called the police. When they arrived they witnessed a young man with a knife in his possession who when they confronted him began to run. One officer stated that they drew their guns and pursued Ben. Ben ran to our house and the officers followed. After explaining to the officers about Ben's disability they seemed understanding, but yet still upset." Later Darrell realized that Ben had only been wearing sweat pants; no shoes or shirt. It was winter and there was snow on the ground.

"What were you trying to do?"

BEN WANTED T PUT BACK TGHYE SOAP NEWSPAPER. It made no sense, but then, this is Ben.

SAD DARING JESSE TIOIGIVE ME CENTS DURING CCREAPY TIMES. (Sad daring Jesse to give me sense - support during creepy times).

When are the times creepy?

NIGBHTIMF (night time)

Why is it creepy then?

BECAUSE I AM SCARED OF BAD NOTIONS ABOUT NOT VFEEHKK,ING SAERE.

Do you mean 'safe'?

YES.

Do you feel unsafe at night because you are afraid you will do something dangerous or because something might happen to you?

DANGERIOUS

What might you do that is dangerous?

CUT CORDS. (Electric cords)

How would you stop yourself?

RESIST CUTTJJING BYSLEEPING XC KINJESSEW BEN (resist cutting by sleeping in Jesse's bed).

• •

Ben needed more security, but we didn't understand that yet. We tried to figure out what was prompting Ben to do these bizarre things. It took time, but slowly we began to realize that Ben engaged in these excursions when he thought he was alone; when no one was there for him at night.

"What should we do about your escaping from the house?"

HIT ME

No. That is not helpful. What else?

GIVE ME ESUPPORT

In the middle of the night? How do we do that?

BE TOUGH FIX THE ALARM

Okay. But do you realize how hard this is for everyone?

SORRY

We still were not thinking about how hard this was for Ben. We installed an alarm system. It seemed like a good start. It also was the end. Ben never left the house again, and the alarm was never set off.

....

A story – The Shower Incident

So, this is a funny story. It wasn't funny when it happened. In fact, it wasn't funny after it happened. As time went bye, however, we began to see how funny it was. And, ultimately, it taught us a lot about seeing things though Ben's eyes.

It began, for Bob and I, about 6-7am with a phone call. We weren't awake yet when the phone rang.

"Sue, this is Jesse. Ben's missing." I sucked in my breath. "Ah, ah, what do you mean he is missing?" I stammered.

"I woke up a few minutes ago." Jesse's voice was calm and flat. "The front door was open. Ben was gone. I called Doc." Doc lived down the street, more than a block and a half away. He was Ben's former teacher in high school, and a good friend of Ben's and our family. Doc hadn't seen Ben, but he also told Jesse that this was his first day of a new job. He couldn't afford to screw it up. "Call the police. Report him as missing. Have you called Sue and Bob? Good grief. Call them!!" He shouted into the phone. "I'll drive around the neighborhood and look for him, but I've got to get to my new job – I can't mess this up." He hung up. Jesse called us.

Normally, it would take us at least 30 minutes to get from our house to Ben's via the interstate. We flew. We were quiet. Each of us was submerged in our personal thoughts of what might have happened to Ben. I don't know about Bob, but I thought of how Ben had been sexually abused in high school. Could some man have captured Ben again and taken him? Would he be a victim again, because of his autism? Would he be prevented from protesting about being violated because he could not speak? Would he be wounded, hurt, victimized – oh. God, the thoughts were heinous.

We arrived at Ben's house feeling desperate and very alone. Jesse met us. His eyes showed us that he was frightened, too. "Darrel and I woke up. The door was open and Ben was gone. We've gone around the block but we can't find him. We called Doc. We don't know where he is." I could feel his desperation and I knew that we had to calm him and give him support so that he didn't feel that his was his fault. We felt desperate and terrified.

"Okay. Let's try to check the neighborhood one more time. Then, if we can't find him, we call the police." This was Bob's calm voice guiding us; giving us hope.

"Jesse, you go around the block again. Sue and I will drive the outer area. We will meet back here and if we can't find him, we will call the police and report him as missing." We agreed and each started off looking, scanning, trying to find a clue about where Ben might be. I bit my lips as I looked into each back yard – would he be there? I would ask myself, knowing that in my heart I was terrified that he might have been abducted. He was so vulnerable, he would go with anyone – or would he? I just didn't know. As we looked for him, was he being abused physically sexually, where the hell was he?????????????

We arrived back at the house. No one was there. We were not sure what to do, but decided we needed to wait for Jesse. It was only a few minutes later that we saw him walking up the street with Ben. They looked like nothing had happened. We waited. The story that Jesse told us, he could not have made this up.

"He was across the street, over there." He pointed to a brown house a few houses down on the other side of the street.

"He was in their shower!" Jesse was smiling, trying not to laugh. Ben was heading up the front stairs and into his house.

Jesse continued.

"I was walking along heading back home when I saw this guy come out onto his front porch with just a towel wrapped around him. I knew immediately where Ben was."

Jesse found Ben coming down the stairs. The guy explained that he thought Ben was one of his housemate's friends, but then he realized Ben was "weird" (his word) and got scared. His housemate wasn't there so he wasn't sure what to do. He had gone out on the porch thinking that his housemate might be out there. Instead he found Jesse. Ben was fine, and very clean.

As each problem situation arose, we all talked about what to do, who should do it, and then we tried to support each other, especially Ben, through the process. We never blamed Ben, we only tried to understand what he was feeling and thinking. Sure, we got frustrated, angry, hurt, but we still understood intuitively that Ben was not totally in control of himself when these things happened. He once typed out that sometimes messages in his body went HAYWIRE. We agreed these were examples of that.

. . . .

A story - Tilt

Ben was around 16-17 when he taught us a valuable lesson about his behavioral issues. He had been facilitating for less than a year and we were still learning how to engage him in conversations. This particular day we were shopping in a large mall. I guess because it was a weekend the mall was pretty crowded. Usually Ben could handle the noise and people, although we were always watching for signs that he was getting too overwhelmed. Ben had a history of hurting himself when he was upset. At the time, we thought this was because of his autism.

Things seemed to be going well as Bob, Ben and I cruised the mall. We decided to head down the escalator to Radio Shack, one of Ben's favorite places. The store was right next to the bottom of the escalator, so down we went. We stepped off the escalator and turned toward Radio Shack. Suddenly, Ben dropped into a sitting position on the floor and began violently slapping the back of his neck – it sounded like a firecracker. He began screaming "No! No!"

It all happened in an instant. Bob and I stared dumbly at each other wondering what had just happened. Our first instinct was to get Ben back on his feet and out of the mall, but that was not going to be easy. Ben was over 6 feet tall and weighed in at a hefty 190 pounds. We simply could not pick him up and carrying him the way we had done when he was younger. "Okay, moving on to Plan B." I thought. That meant helping Ben to get back some self-control. I knew from experience that, once Ben was this out of control, he would not be able to regain control without help.

I quickly sat down beside Ben on the floor. I didn't touch him or try to restrain him. I knew this would only escalate an already deteriorating situation.

"Wow Ben. You took me by surprise. My guess is something really upset you, but we can talk about that later." I spoke quietly and looked up at Bob. Already a curious crowd of on-lookers was beginning to gather.

"Oh shit." I thought. "I know what is probably going to happen next." As if on cue, I could see a security guard rapidly approaching, his hand on his holster.

"Bob, I have Ben. You have him." And I jerked my head toward the guard. I turned to Ben.

"Okay, beautiful guy. I need your help here. I am not sure what to do to help you right now." As I was saying this I pulled out Ben's communication device – a little electronic memo maker that we had actually bought at Radio Shack. I had a fleeting silly thought – "...guess they wouldn't want to use this scene as part of their advertising." I would have chuckled, but actually I was sweating and feeling pretty nervous. I needed to keep control of myself, so I asked Ben to help me.

Even though these thoughts took barely seconds, all the while Ben was slapping his neck and screaming "No! No!" I looked at Bob who was talking calmly to the security guard, but the guard didn't look happy. The crowd was closing in around us. I could feel the sweat rolling down my forehead and back. I decided to ask Ben a series of questions that he could answer Yes or No. "Let's keep it simple." I thought.

"Ben, should I tell you to stop?" His right hand shot out and with his index finger extended he jabbed at the N on the keyboard. His left hand was busy slapping. He was beginning to breathe quickly and I could see the tears beginning to form in his eyes. "Quick," I thought. "Move on."

"Should I talk softly?" Again Ben's hand shot out and he typed Y. "Great." I thought.

"We are communicating. That's a start."

"Should we stand up?" N

"Can you get control?" N

Beautiful Ben

"Can you stop slapping yourself?" N

"Should I keep asking questions?" Y

"Is this helping you?" Y [How come your are still slapping yourself and screaming No? I wanted to ask this, but knew I shouldn't. Ben was starting to cry. I felt like crying too.

"Do you want Dad to talk with you?" N

"I am not sure what I should do, Ben. Can you tell me what you need?" Y

"Great!! What should I do?" [I felt a bit of relief, but it was fleeting. I looked at Bob. He was standing now between the security guard and Ben and I. His feet were firmly planted and his arms were outstretched slightly. It looked like he was gesturing a "what else can I do?" query, but I also knew he was trying to prevent the guard from getting too close to Ben. We both knew this would not end well if that happened, and I, for one, didn't want to get arrested.

I rephrased my question.

"What should I do?" Ben briefly hesitated and then with sharp jabbing strokes, he quickly spelled out "HIT ME." His slapping was getting harder. His tears were spilling off his chin. He was beginning to pinch his side with his right hand.

"Ben" I pleaded. "I can't hit you. I just can't. And certainly I can't hit you in front of all these people and with a policeman watching. Be real." I was beginning to panic. I suddenly realized that no one, least of all the cop, would understand that Ben was our son. He is black; we are white. He is adopted. Right now, however, none of that mattered.

"What else can I do?" I was frantically thinking of questions. If I could keep the conversation going, maybe, just maybe, he would tire out and stop.

Suddenly, he began typing with fast sharp motions. "LIKE A RECORD PLAYER."

"Like a record player?" I repeated. I was dumbfounded, but then I suddenly realized what he was asking me to do.

"Okay, beautiful guy. Here goes." I let go of Ben's hand and with the heel of my right hand I hit his left shoulder and said "tilt." Before I could blink, Ben's hands dropped to his side and he got to his feet.

Without looking at me or Bob he began quickly walking away from us, down the mall. I was still sitting on the floor with my hand up in the air. I had to no time to process what had just happened.

"Bob. Ben is on his way." I scrambled to my feet and began to follow Bob as he followed Ben. I looked at the security guard who was standing with his hands on his hips looking totally bewildered. As I walked away, I heard him say, "Okay, folks. Show's over. Go on about your business." I guess he had to do something official. I caught up with Ben and Bob as they were leaving the mall. We went to our car and drove home in silence. I know that each of us was thinking about what had just happened, but we needed time before we could talk about it.

A few days later, I asked Ben to tell me what had happened.

"NOT WANT TO GO TO RADIO SHACK. RESIST LOSING CONTROL. FUCKED UP."

"You didn't fuck up, Ben. And you are not fucked up. You did lose control, but you also got over it. You could tell me how to help. That was the most important thing that happened. I'm proud of you that you could tell me what to do. It sure helped me stay in control. You did that. You helped me stay in control."

"How did my hitting you and saying 'tilt' help?

"STUCK HITTING. COULD NOT STOP.

Are you telling me that you were stuck? You kept slapping yourself because you were stuck and could not stop?

Y

Did my hitting your shoulder and saying 'tilt' get you unstuck?"

Y

That was the end of our conversation, but I had learned a lot from it.

• •

As I reflected on this episode and what Ben typed later, I came to several conclusions. First, it wasn't Ben's autism that caused him to slap himself and scream at himself, it was his inability to communicate to us what he wanted and needed. My guess is that we didn't talk about going to Radio Shack, we just assumed that Ben wanted to go. We didn't ask him. I'm not sure why he didn't want to go, but I do know we treated him like a child and didn't respect that he could make a choice for himself.

Beautiful Ben

Another insight was about Ben's asking me to hit him. It had never occurred to me that he might be stuck like that, like a record, as he put it. From that time on, we would ask Ben if he was stuck and if he indicated yes, we would gently hit his shoulder, just as we had done that day, and say "tilt". It didn't always work, but just the act of asking him, engaging him in managing his own behavior, started us all on a gentler path.

Ben's behavior has been an ongoing source of consternation, conversation and attention over the years. He has hurt himself - "self-injurious behavior" the psychologists called it - pinching his sides and face until they bled, cutting himself with knives, vehemently slapping his face and neck until he raised welts and bruises. He has destroyed property, he has disappeared unexpectedly, he has cried, bounced, engaged in repetitive rocking, finger flapping or "self-stimming" motions. He has never smeared his feces - small blessing, but I'll take it. Why has he done these things? I am not sure, but I have some hypotheses, some ideas, hunches.

First, and it has taken me a long time to realize this - Ben does not want people to control or restrain him. He fights his oppressor and he fights himself. The feeling of being restrained, the physical touch alone, is so hurtful and aversive to him, he reacts. He fights in the only way he knows. He hurts himself. He beats up on himself for not being able to fight back.

MY UPSETS ARE JHUST HATEFUL.

'I am sure they make you feel horrible. What strategies help you to feel calm and happy?'

LOVE ME.

'That is easy for me, but what about strategies for others who haven't gotten to know you well yet?'

MY FRIENDS PLPPLOT EACH THINKG WITH ME.

Ben was explaining how important it is for people to plan carefully to help him avoid situations that will provoke him and, if they truly care about him, they will give him the kind of support he needs for each situation, as best they can.

Second, his body physically does not react to sounds, lights, visions, perceptions, smells, in the same way as other peoples' do. He has typed out that sometimes his thoughts go HAYWIRE and his body reacts in ways he doesn't mean. The incident at Radio Shack illustrates this. As we descended on the escalator there was a mirror straight ahead. The lights were shining, sparkling, reflecting. He could not handle these. These reflections literally drove him crazy and he lost control. He just couldn't help it. Had we been more observant, we might have realized that this mirror could spark an upset feeling in Ben. Possibly we could have avoided the entire episode. Who knows?

Third, sometimes people say things or act in certain ways that offend Ben. He gets upset, frustrated, angry, but because he cannot talk or communicate these feelings in traditional ways, he "loses" it. He wants to yell "You asshole! You jerk! How would you like it if someone called you a 'retard' or a 'weirdo' or a 'wacko' and you could not fight back?" But Ben can't do that, and he doesn't. He blames himself for losing control, which only makes things worse.

Once, when he acted really stupidly, Jesse accused him of "living down to that man's expectations of you". Of course, he was right, but Ben hates it when people expect him to be "autistic."

GOT ME UPS4T BECAUWE ...THE TREATING IS YUCH.

WE JUST REALLY GOT ON EWACH TOHRS NERVS. SAD ABOYHGB (about) REFUSING.

Fourth, Ben can control some of his actions and he likes to know he can. It is his declaration of control.

"Ben, why do you keep saying 'And you can cry. And you can cry?'

BEN LIKES IRRITATING MOM. He's good at it, too.

Finally, and most important, Ben wants desperately to be able to control his body - his "behavior" as others label it.

HQATE HFEEKLIHG NJTYRHY JE4R JERKY. (Hate feeling jerky).

It's taken me awhile to realize that, all along, we have been asking Ben the wrong question. It's not really so important why he did something - he probably doesn't know either. What really is important to ask is what do you, Ben, need to feel safe, loved, okay? That is the important question, and it is the question Ben can answer. In doing so he gives us what we need, the right thing to do.

Normal, what ever that is, just doesn't exist for us anymore. Somehow, Darrell and Jesse were able to develop a good relationship, a friendship with Ben despite his oddities. They just seemed to be able to figure out how to make this all work. Granted we spent a lot of time problem solving and talking with each other and Ben about what was best, but they genuinely cared about Ben and his well-being. That is what made the difference.

Jesse, Jesse, Jesse

When Darrell left at the end of that first year we were sad to see him go, but also so happy that Jesse wanted to stay. He continued to live with Ben for the next ten years. They became the best of friends and Bob and I developed a profound relationship with Jesse. He became part of our family. In fact, we often referred to him as our "acquired son." His own family was dysfunctional, to say the least, and he had minimal contact with them. His sisters visited occasionally, and one brother stayed briefly with him and Ben.

Jesse was totally charming. Everyone who met him liked him, well almost everyone. He was handsome and fun loving and willing to try new things. He deeply cared about Ben and Ben reciprocated this affection and respect. Jesse wasn't very good at getting and keeping jobs, however. He tried attending the local community college, but that didn't work either. He just couldn't seem to find what he wanted. This was true for his girl friends too. Over the years he had a number of girl friends, some we met, some we didn't. One or two were definitely interested in marriage, but that was not on Jesse's radar. He was always clear that he and Ben were a package too. When he started dating Jenn, she was happy to be with Ben. She was a free spirited young woman who also was insecure. Jesse helped her feel better about herself, and she helped him focus.

· ·

A story – Jenn, camping, and a bad acid trip

Jenn was probably one of the best things that ever happened to Jesse and Ben. Jesse met Jenn at a sleazy bar and they "hit it off.' At the time, she went by the name of MJ (short for MariJuana). It wasn't long before she moved into Ben and Jesse's house. But this story is about a camping trip they took in the summer after she moved in. She had arranged it. For a few years before moving in with Ben and Jesse she had become part of the "Rainbow Coalition" and had participated in their annual campouts. This year the campout was in northern Pennsylvania and she convinced Jesse and Ben to go.

This story is about something that happened there. My version may not be totally accurate, but I think it does capture the essence of what happened – at least as they told me about it later.

They arrived at the campsite and set up their camp. The accepted rule was that everything was to be peaceful and laid back. There probably was a lot of pot smoking too, but the main thing was to relax, have fun, and enjoy. For those who wanted too, also It was acceptable to be nude. No one made a big deal about it. Ben decided he wanted to be nude, but Jenn and Jesse chose not to. That was okay.

On the second night, however, something really upset Ben. Who knows what. He started slapping his face, his neck, his head. Jesse and Jenn tried to calm him down, but were totally unsuccessful. He only became more agitated and upset. Two guys from the next campsite filtered over.

"Hey man, what's going on?" one of the guys asked. Jesse explained that Ben was upset, "not sure why" and that he and Jenn were having a hard time trying to calm him down. The two guys sat down with Ben. They didn't say much. They just sat with him. Jenn and Jesse drifted off, happy that they had a break. They didn't know the guys, but trusted that, because they were part of the Rainbow Coalition, they would be okay with Ben.

Later, Jenn and Jesse came back. Ben was sleeping and the two guys were sitting quietly nearby. "Hey man," said Jesse, "Thanks." He shook their hands. "No big deal man." One of the guys said. "We know what it is like to have a bad acid trip. We've been there. Just wanted to help."

An acid trip??? Ben hadn't had an acid trip – he had had an autism trip, but he was okay. He was safe. He was supported. He was accepted. It is all about your perspective.

· ·

Jenn moved in and shortly after became pregnant with twins. They asked us to be the grandparents and we were thrilled. Ben loved Jenn, too. Sometimes he got jealous of Jesse and protective of Jenn, but he was thrilled when they asked him to name one of the twins. The boys were born full term, but one of them struggled in the beginning. It was a tense time for all of us, but eventually he came home from the hospital and life began to settle - or so we thought.

I'm not sure what happened, but one night Jenn called to tell me that she and the boys were moving out. She just couldn't handle the way Jesse was acting. She felt torn, especially for Ben, because she cared so much for him and she loved Jesse, but she felt she had to leave. She moved home with her mother.

Jesse seemed to flounder after this. He couldn't keep a job and he seemed to become increasingly depressed. When we tried to talk to him about his, he refused.

"I'm fine! I am not depressed!" He didn't shout this, but it was clear he was not going to discuss anything. We offered counseling or anything he needed that would be helpful, but he still refused. "It was the best of times. It was the worst of times." as Charles Dickens said.

Jesse seemed to slowly shut down. Today I would say he was probably bi-polar, but at the time I could only see how much he was hurting. We wanted to help, but he rebuked us at every turn. Ben was suffering too, but he wanted to be with Jesse. One day, Jesse called. He wanted to come out to our house.

"Sue, I want to talk to you". I was hopeful that finally things would change. He and I had a very special friendship and I hoped he was finally going to let me into his tormented thoughts. I was wrong. We were sitting out on the front deck watching Ben swim. It was warm and sunny. I waited. This was Jesse's agenda.

"Sue. I have to leave." His voice was flat. I sucked in my breath and held it. This was not what I had expected. I didn't say anything. I couldn't.

"I have to know I can live on my own. I have lived with Ben for almost ten years. I have never lived on my own. I need to know I can do that." There was a finality in his voice that was chilling.

"Can we talk about this? Have you talked to Ben about this? Where would you go?" My mind was flooded with questions. I tried to calm myself, but my heart and my mind were going berserk. I suddenly felt chilled. I looked out at Ben and wondered what he would do. How would we manage? What would happen?

Jesse was talking. "I'll go out west to my brother's." He made it sound so simple, but I knew he had already convinced himself. I couldn't speak. I was fighting the tears and the silent scream that was rising in my chest. How can you walk away from Ben, from us like this? We are your family. We love you. These were my thoughts. I didn't have to say them, Jesse knew.

We sat there for a while, not speaking. Finally, my voice tight in my throat, I said, "Is there anything I can do to make you change your mind, to make you stay?" I heard the desperation in my voice. He didn't answer right away. The silence was thick. I began to sweat. Finally, in a deep and quiet voice he simply said "No. I need to do this."

Time passed and finally I asked him to leave. I just didn't know what else to say or do. I needed time to think. He left, and within two weeks he was packed and gone. He was there one day, and the next, he simply had vanished. He didn't tell anyone where he was going or what he was going to do. We didn't hear from him for the next several years. He called once to ask for money. I don't know where he was.

Stupidly I wired him $100 but told him to never call again if he was only going to ask for money. Of course, I didn't hear from him. Neither did Ben. He was devastated, hurt, angry. He typed that Jesse had told him he was leaving, but he never said what that meant to him or how he felt. He missed Jesse. We all did.

I PULLK UP THJOUGGHTAS PALV (I pull up thoughts of pals.)

"Palv??"

PALS

"Which pals?

JESSE

"These are old thoughts. Jesse is gone and he will not come back."

HE IS HERE AT TIMES. HE UIS IN MY MIND.

What do we do now?

Suddenly we had this huge house, but Ben couldn't stay there alone. Jesse had been there so long and now Ben had nothing. We brought Ben home.

I QUESTION WHERE I AM GOIING TO LIVE.

He wanted to stay in his house, but without people to support him, how could he? I also think, now, that I needed Ben to be with us. I wanted to soften the hurt, to make him feel safe, to help him. Who was I fooling? I wanted these things. Jesse had deeply hurt Bob and I as well.

We met with people at the agency. What were our options? What could we do? They scheduled a meeting with the Residential Coordinator so that we could begin the process of finding a new housemate. It seemed so bureaucratic, but we knew this was what we needed to do. We had to move on, but it was so hard!!

We had never met Barry, the Residential Coordinator, but he listened to our story and what Ben wanted. It was shaky, but we knew we had to move forward. Barry agreed to place ads in the local paper and to investigate people who had previously applied to the agency as potential roommates. At home, we tried to establish a normal routine, to make Ben feel safe and a part of our home, but it was strained. He had a hard time sleeping; so did we. He needed something to do during the day; his work had been totally disrupted.

At the time Jesse left, Ben had been working on building birdhouses and wooden tables. We had built a small shop in his basement. Different people had been hired by the agency to work with Ben. Usually they lasted a month or two. Some left because they could not handle Jesse's control of Ben and the house.

Beautiful Ben

Others left because they could not work with Ben. They said they didn't think it was safe for him to work with power tools. They were afraid he would get hurt. They were also afraid that Ben would hurt them. Some simply didn't have the necessary skills. Bob and I were convinced that Ben needed to continue his daily work. He felt good about what he did and he wanted to work, so we made it happen. Every morning, we would drive Ben to his house to work and then pick him up later in the afternoon to bring him back to our house. It wasn't ideal, but we believed it was right.

How do we find new housemates?

Another meeting with the agency was scheduled. Barry began the meeting by telling us that he had interviewed several potential housemates, but there was a problem.

"Oh shit." I thought. Here we go again. "What kind of problem?" I asked.

Barry began slowly. "I have interviewed several people, but I feel a real conflict of interest. You see, I would like to be Ben's house mate." He looked at us and waited. "What am I supposed to say to that?" I thought. I didn't know this person and I had no idea if Ben knew him either. I really was at a loss. I knew Bob felt the same.

Before I could say anything, however, Barry continued. "My girl friend and I have talked about life sharing for some time. We want to do that. We just haven't found the right person yet. I've told her about Ben. He and I know each other from here (the agency). She wants to meet Ben and if it is alright with you two, she and I would like to spend some time with him to see if this might work." He waited for us to digest this new idea. We didn't know what to say. I could tell he was serious, but I had no idea what Ben might say. I didn't know what they expected, either, but I believed that if he worked for this agency he must be invested with the right values. We agreed to move slowly and see what Ben wanted.

Barry and his girl friend Brianne took time to get to know Ben. He seemed to like them. They were young, around his age, and she also worked for a disability agency as a job coach. It seemed like an okay match and Ben was up for trying. No one from the agency cautioned us. We agreed to have them move in with Ben when their current lease was up.

We were fools. We should have been more thorough and careful. It didn't take long for Ben's Lancaster house to become Barry and Brianne's house, with Ben as the guest. They brought their cats and a dog and their pet reptiles. Snakes and lizards have never bothered me so this wasn't a problem at first. Ben seemed to be happy and he didn't mind the animals. At least he didn't complain about them.

Six months went bye. Bob and I began our new semester of classes and hoped that Ben's life would be better. We trusted the agency to provide oversight. I had just gotten my first cell phone when I got a frantic call from Barry.

The house is on fire!

"Sue, the house is on fire. Our house is burning. It's burning. Oh my god!" I could hear the fear in his voice. "I just got home from work and there was smoke and flames and, and I went in the back door, and and .... Ben's okay. He wasn't here. The house is burning. Oh my god. The fire department is here. Oh god...I, I... wait, wait. I'll call you right back." Click. The cell phone went dead.

So did I. I waited not knowing what to do. The phone rang. It was Barry. His voice was still scared and frantic. "Sue, Ben came home. He saw the fire. I told Doug to take him away. He'll call you later." Barry was crying. So was I.

"Sue, Sue, wait, the fire marshal has to talk to you." I could hear him passing the phone to someone as he told them that I was the house's owner.

"Mrs. Lehr, this is the city fire marshal. The house fire is under control. We have a company here that can board it up temporarily. No one can stay here. It is not safe. Call me tomorrow and we will meet to discuss what to do." He gave the phone back to Barry who was still distraught. I knew intuitively I needed to be the voice of reason, of sanity even though I felt like screaming.

"Barry, I will call Doug and arrange to get Ben. I will take him to Tully. You and Brianne can stay there too until we figure out what to do.

"I need to go see about our cats and our dog. The guy next door took the snakes. I have to find him. I'll call you later." And he hung up. I felt numb, but I knew I had to find Bob. We had to get Ben. I went to the building where Bob was holding his class and I walked the halls looking in each classroom until I found him. As I walked in the classroom I recognized many of the students. They smiled and greeted me.

"Bob, I need to speak to you immediately. There has been an emergency." My voice was calm and constrained. I looked at Bob and motioned to the door. He kind of chuckled and, nodding to the students said, "My wife. You never know what's happening in our family," and followed me out the door. I quickly told him about the fire. He stepped back into the classroom and told his students, "Ben's house has burned. He is okay, but we need to go." The students were shocked.

"Are you sure he is okay? Can we do anything? What do you need?" I thought I would cry. They were so genuine and supportive. We told them we would let everyone know what was happening as soon as we knew and we left campus. On route to Ben's house we called Doug, his current support person. He told us that he and Ben had arrived home just as the fire trucks arrived. Barry had told Doug to get Ben out of there so Doug had taken Ben to his house and then on to get his wife at work. They had stopped at McDonald's on the way home; Doug thought that might calm Ben.

My mind was a chaos of thoughts. Had anyone explained to Ben what was happening? Were Barry and Brianne okay? What shape was the house in? What would we do? We drove to Doug's and found Ben waiting for us in his car. He was quite agitated. Barry called to say the fire marshal had approved the boarding up of the house. There was nothing else we could do. He said Brianne was going to stay with her aunt or cousin. Barry wanted to come and stay with us for the night, but he had to take his dog to his mother's...I am not sure what happened after that. It was a whirlwind, a tornado of devastation.

Bob had just been diagnosed with Alzheimer's two weeks before the fire, and we were still reeling from this. He didn't want anyone to know, but the fire distracted us anyway. We had immediate needs of dealing with a burned out house, Ben's fears, Barry and Brianne's needs as housemates, insurance issues, work, on and on. Wine became our drug of choice. At night we would sit and problem solve. By day we met our classes, talked with our "big loss" insurance agent (who was a dream come true) and tried to cope with Bob's diagnosis and what that meant.

We can't think straight

First we needed, once again, to figure out what would happen for Ben. We were fragile, shaky, scared. We took a breath. We knew we needed to think through what we should do. Before we could do this, however, Barry and Brianne said that they wanted to move into an apartment and Ben could stay with them. He wanted to do this, although I had fleeting memories of his thoughts about apartment living years ago. He wanted to help us too, and we thought we should agree with his decision.

Barry and Brianne chose an apartment complex where they had lived before, but it was quite a distance away. They thought it was perfect because they could keep their two cats. Their dog could stay with Barry's parents. The reptiles were staying at a pet store. It was a two-bedroom apartment on the first floor. The insurance had paid for Ben to have some new clothes so we packed these and helped Ben move. Our insurance also helped to pay the rent on this new apartment. I don't know what went wrong, but this new arrangement just didn't work. We would get phone calls from Barry at different times of the night - 2 AM, 4 AM - whenever.

Sue Lehr

"Ben's having a really hard time. I don't mean to ask you for help, but I am afraid I will have a seizure." He never specifically asked for us to come and get Ben, but I could hear it in his voice. Bob and I also knew that if Ben was that out of control, slapping himself, screaming, crying, he needed help and he needed it now. We would drive the 45 minutes, twice though horrible snowstorms, to get there. Ben would be out of control, violently slapping himself and screaming "No Ben, stop that! Stop that!" It was awful. Barry would tell us how awful it had been for them, too." We tried to make them feel better, but our real concern was for Ben. We moved him home. We needed to think.

It is time to retire

Just two weeks prior to the fire, Bob had been diagnosed with early on-set Alzheimer's Disease. We had not suspected such a dreadful outcome of the testing he had been going through. We were stunned and numb.

"Bob, we have to retire. I don't care if we don't tell anyone why, but we have to do this." He agreed. We told our colleagues that Bob had a serious health problem. Thankfully, no one asked for details. They respected that we needed privacy.

Ben was staying with us, although occasionally he stayed at the apartment. We talked about building a new house on some land we owned out in the country near where we lived. We had originally bought the land so Penny, her boyfriend and their infant daughter, Daniele, could build a house there. Brian was killed in a snow mobile accident when Daniele was eight months old. She and Penny moved home with us after that. We kept the property so it seemed perfect for building a new home for Ben. I felt like I was going crazy. I wanted to talk to Jesse, but he was gone. We had to figure this out ourselves. It was truly, the worst of times.

The Cardiff House

The land we owned was in the town of Cardiff. We would take Ben there and talk about building a new house for him, and a shop where he could build his furniture. We needed hope and this became our dream. Before Jesse left, he and Ben had talked about building a modular home out in the country, maybe on the "Cardiff land". Maybe it was time. We talked to Barry and Brianne about this idea. They liked it and, with Ben, they began to plan. They looked at floor plans and ultimately decided on what they wanted. It was not what Ben, Jesse, Bob and I had originally planned, but we thought it was what Ben wanted. He decided on the interior decor, siding colors, rugs and a few other details. We put the Lancaster house up for sale and began the negotiations for this new Cardiff home.

Beautiful Ben

We contracted with a builder friend to pour the foundation and oversee the construction of the new house. Fortunately, the housing market was at a real peak and we were able to sell the Lancaster house at a good price, but not without some sticky back and forth about repairs. Our real estate agent was a close friend (Pat Floyd's husband). He made sure that we were not being abused. The closing on the house was cause for a celebration since that assured our being able to buy the new modular house. A date was set for placing the house on the foundation and we all cheered. Bob and I were hopeful that, finally, Ben's life would be stable.

Near the end of the summer, Ben's Cardiff house was positioned on the foundation. It took a few weeks after that to finish the siding, roof, electricals and such, but the progress was fun and we all knew it would be ready soon. Once again, we helped Ben pack. A moving date was set and Ben, Barry, Brianne and all their pets moved in. It didn't take long, however, for things to deteriorate. When Bob and I visited the house we were upset to find the living room being the used as the "reptile" room. There were three or four cages along the walls housing their snakes and lizards. Nothing in the room belonged to Ben. The cats' cages and the dog's crate were also in this room.

"Oh my god. Look at that." I pointed to the lights on top of the cages. "They're not fastened down. They could be knocked off easily. This can't happen again." I was shaking. The cause of the Lancaster house fire had been determined by the fire marshal as having been started by a heat lamp from one of the reptile cages. He said that the lamp had probably been dislodged or knocked onto the floor. Left unattended, it had eventually ignited the floor, carpeting, and/or the curtains. We all assumed that the cats had probable knocked the lamp over. We tried not to point blame, but we could not have this situation repeat itself.

"Barry, you have to fasten down those lamps. This is dangerous. Please, please fix this." I was pleading. Later, Barry would tell us that we had no right to tell him how to take care of his animals.

Then, one day, Penny stopped to visit Ben. She had not been feeling good about how Barry acted around Ben. She just wanted to be sure Ben was okay. She sensed that Ben was tense and unhappy.

When she arrived, a friend of Ben's was there. Barry and Brianne were at work. Ben's friend said he was upstairs in his room so Penny went up. She was shocked, stunned, disgusted to find piles of dried dog poop, "Dog shit, Mom!" on the floor in Ben's bedroom. She asked Dave, Ben's friend who was there every afternoon to support Ben, how this had happened. Dave told her that Barry had instructed him, and Ben's other support people, that they were not permitted to go upstairs.

"That is our private living quarters. Stay out." Evidently everyone obeyed, but not Penny. She was furious. She, Ben and Dave cleaned up the rugs, but they also found evidence of cat pee in several locations in Ben's bedroom. By the time Penny was finished cleaning, she was livid with anger. As if this was not enough, later she discovered that there was a mouse-breeding cage in the front hall closet. The mice were the food for the reptiles. She opened the closet and was overwhelmed with the smell. She found rodent hairs and feces on the coats, Ben's coats, and on the floor. She reported this to the agency and waited for Barry to come home. She told him, in no uncertain terms, that he had to clean up the mouse breeding cages, fasten the lights on the reptile cages, and restrict his cats. He didn't accept this well.

His dog was usually in the crate when any of us visited. When he was out, however, he was not well behaved. He had lunged at me several times and later we learned his dog had bitten one of Ben's friends. Ben has never been an animal person, but this was getting out of hand. I also called the agency and Barry. He didn't like our interference.

Ben was saying things that made us worry about his safety. "You sit in that chair. I'll tie you in that chair. I'll lock the door." It was scary. I wanted to believe they were good people, that they treated Ben well, but I had lost my faith in them. We told them they had to leave. We gave them three months. We said we just didn't think this was working for anyone. They agreed to leave, but the date came and went and they had not left. They said they were buying a house and they were just waiting for the closing date to be set. We waited, but still they didn't leave. Ben was miserable. I didn't think they would hurt him, and he wanted to stay in his own house. It was horrible. The closing date came and went and still they were there so we said they had to leave or we would evict them. They said they would leave the following week.

All the while, the agency was overseeing what was happening. We were confident they were protecting Ben, but they could not be there all the time. They also had begun to look for new housemates for Ben. In the meantime, Bob, Penny and I tried to be there as much as we could. One day, Bob and I stopped to visit. Ben was working in his shop. Barry was there with Brianne's cousin. They were packing and moving boxes into Barry's car.

"We'll be out of here by the end of the week." Barry said flatly, never looking directly at me.

"We're just packing some things now for storage." I nodded and told him that Bob and I would be back later after Ben finished work. We left.

Beautiful Ben

When we returned a few hours later, the house had been stripped. All of Ben's living room furniture was gone along with a number of other items - lamps, computers, the television, kitchen items. We were shocked, horrified actually. I immediately called the local police and reported the theft. The police officer who arrived knew Ben. It was a comfort. We explained the situation. She interviewed Ben's support person who remembered the moving van company's name. Within hours most of the stolen items had been located and returned. Barry and Brianne protested that these items belonged to them and eventually filed a small claims court action against us. I had receipts for what we had bought after the fire so their efforts at extorting money from us failed. We prevailed, but we had learned a bitter lesson about trust. The folks at Onondaga Community living arranged for people to stay with Ben so that he could continue to live in his own house. We all took it one day at a time, and life moved on.

Ben welcomes Johnny

Barry and Brianne were gone. Now who would live with Ben? We began the hunting process again. The agency put ads in the paper. This time, however, we said they had to handle the screening process. We trusted them. They knew Ben. They understood him. Several different staff members had spent a lot of time with Ben, supporting him, staying over night, being with him. This time they had a much better sense of what Ben needed. Bob and I also began to realize that we had to withdraw from being so involved in Ben's life. We were/are getting older. Bob had his good days, and he also had some bad ones. We needed to know that Ben could be okay if we weren't there. We knew that Penny would always be there for Ben, but she had her family too. We wanted to feel confident that if we died, "got hit by a bus" as my insurance agent kept saying, that Ben would be okay.

Angelo, who worked with Ben and his furniture building business, suggested to Ben that his friend, Johnny, might be a good housemate. Ben knew Johnny through Angelo. For the first time in our lives, we stepped back. We said to Angelo, the agency, and Ben, "You decide. We can't do this anymore. It has to be what will work for Ben and you all have to be sure this is right. We can't." They understood we weren't abandoning Ben. They understood that Ben and we trusted them, and Ben needed people he could trust and who would respect him. Johnny had a good job and seemed to like being with Ben. We were confident that Brian, Ben's residential service coordinator and friend, and Angelo would be vigilant. They deeply cared about Ben and didn't want to see him hurt again.

Although it was a little rough in the beginning, Johnny and Ben were housemates for over a year. They developed a friendship and it appeared that things were going smoothly. We all knew that Johnny had some of his own family problems, but he kept these pretty much to himself. The agency continued to provide the wrap around supports and supervision. Bob and I relaxed. We didn't have to be involved in the day-to-day machinations of Ben's life. We would stop and visit periodically, and we continued to have him come and visit, generally one weekend a month. We were beginning to feel that life for Ben was going to be okay. We trusted the people around Ben to keep us informed if anything didn't seem right. Later, we all agreed that we just didn't see what was about to happen, and we could not understand it.

A story – Belt welts

I was surprised to see Johnny and Ben pull in our driveway. It was a warm and sunny Saturday, but we had not planned on Ben visiting. Ben got out of the car and my first reaction was he looked scared. He was pale and very tentative.

"I want to borrow the lawn mower. Okay?" Johnny hurried around the back of the car and sprung open the trunk. "I have to cut the grass today."

"Would you like to stay here for a while, Ben?"

STAY IN TULLY, YES.

I looked at Ben. His voice was soft, weak sounding. He looked like he was pleading with me. Intuitively, I knew something was wrong. I watched as Johnny loaded the lawn mower into the trunk of his car. He looked scared too. What was going on?

"Johnny, would you like Ben to stay here while you cut the grass? We could take him home later." He nodded his head and quickly got into the driver's seat and left.

Ben wanted to go swimming in the lake so off he went to get his suit on. Within minutes he was in the lake. When he got out I went out on the dock to chat with him, but I was stopped in my tracks when I saw a large red welt on his shoulder. As I looked at it, I noticed other raised welts in the shape of a belt buckle, a large one, on Ben's arms and the backs of his legs.

There was a similar bruise on Ben's left side of his back at waist level. It was inflamed. We went inside and when Ben removed his bathing suit, we found cuts, other welts, and bruises on the back of his thighs, each about 4 inches long, that looked like a strap mark. The welts were turning purple. Ben was visibly upset and began swearing and hurting himself.

"Ben, what happened? What is going on?" Of course, I was asking about the bruises, but Ben had other thoughts.

WISH ICOULD STOP SAYING FUCKTO Y OU..

Is there anything I can do to help you stop?

ORDER BEN WIK WG TO STOP.

I order Ben to stop swearing!!! Right now!!!

GOOD.

I tried to stay calm. I asked Ben who had hit him? At first he refused to answer, but later he told us that Johnny had beaten him with his belt. We also learned that this wasn't the first time. I took Ben to his doctor who photographed the marks and reported the abuse. I called the agency and also reported what had happened. Johnny was removed from the house within hours. His defense was that he was stressed. I'll never know, nor do I care, why he never asked for help. Brian and Angelo were there everyday, but Johnny had not said a word.

• •

There has to be a better way.

Lauren, Ben's Service Coordinator, immediately called a meeting of Ben's support team. We talked for a long time and we all agreed that Ben needed time to recover, time in his own home without worrying about what might happen to him. Brian arranged for different people to stay with Ben in the afternoons and overnight. Ben knew these people and felt safe with them. Now, more than a year later, Ben seems happier than he has been in a long time. He has finally gotten his original wish, to live alone. He has different friends who are there to help him, but he sets the schedule and rhythm of his life. He is calm and I think he is content.

Penny and Dee decided to buy the house next door to Ben's when it went on the market last fall. They wanted to live near him. It took a while to arrange the financing, but they are settling in. Ben loves having them so close. He wanders over when he wants to see them, and they are at his house daily. The kids love their Uncle Ben, and he loves them as well. Life is good, at least for now. But as Bob says every day, "One day at a time."

Chapter 18

This is not the last chapter, but it will do for now

As Bob and I face our own ending, our ultimate death, we have to think about what we should do to protect Ben's future, our life for as long as it may happen, and Penny and Sherry's life. As Bob's Alzheimer's creeps more perniciously into his brain, we must face what will happen. Each night at about 5 PM we have our "wine time". Our bodies are tired from what we have done during the day, and now it is time to allow our brains to decompress. We talk, sometimes for hours, but usually for an hour to an hour and a half. We begin with a glass of chilled white wine. We have been through so much and we do feel, despite all, it has been a good life. We live one day at a time, but we also have planned for our future. When we die, which we will some day, who will be there for Ben?

An essay – Who Will Be There When We Are Not?

Who will know? Who will understand? Who will care?

These are the questions I ask myself each day as things happen in Ben's life and ours.

Who will be there when he gets agitated or beats himself up, to understand that he might be sick, maybe he has a headache, or is stressed, or wants to say something? Who will care enough to try to find out what is going on? Who will know that restraining him is the worse thing you can do? Who will care that he is trying to tell you something? Who will care at all?

Who will know that his verbal words are only part of what he has to say. Who will know that he wants to facilitate something? Who will know how to facilitate with him? Who will care to take the time to do this thoughtfully, carefully, sensitively?

Who will understand that he can cut his own toenails and finger nails without hurting himself with the clippers. Who will care? Who will take away the clippers? Who will understand this is a matter of independence and dignity.

Who will help him shave his face and his head? Personal grooming is important to Ben. He likes his head shaved – why? He thinks he looks cool. He won't try to pull out his hair when he is upset if his head is shaved. He likes the feeling of having his head shaved. He loves it when people tell him he looks "cool." Who will give him the

Beautiful Ben

personal autonomy to try to shave himself – face and head, and then offer to "do a little touching up," without demeaning him? Who will care?

Who will know that he likes albacore white tuna with Hellmann's mayonnaise and finely diced celery and onions. Who will think to ask if he wants this in a bowl or in a sandwich?

Who will understand that his allergies to dairy products don't prohibit him forever eating a piece of cheese or chocolate? He knows what his body can tolerate and, if given the chance, will generally restrict himself. But just like all of us who know we shouldn't eat something, chocolate, fats, whatever, he needs the chance to be human. Who will care enough to help him set his own limits? Who will understand when to intervene?

Who will know how much Ben likes to play his keyboard and his Blue Man? Who will know when he is reaching that point of obsession where he cannot turn it off himself? Who will be there to help him? Who will help him download his favorite music to his iPod and remind him how to scroll to the music he wants?

Who will set reasonable limits for Ben that respect him, cherish his independence, and imply a sense of collaboration, not domination and control?

Who will allow him to wear the clothes he wants. He likes to wear sweat pants and short-sleeved T-shirts. He hates jeans because the zipper rubs on his penis and this arouses him. Who will understand this? He loves to look well dressed, but the choice of clothes has to be his. He loves to shop and will pick out good things, but who will allow him this autonomy?

One of Ben's favorite foods is rare/medium steak, especially cooked on the grille. Who will care how it is cooked? Who will allow him the privilege of cutting his own meat with a steak knife, a sharp one? Who will understand that cutting chicken, another favorite, from the bone is difficult? Who will care that he might need a little help with this, but that he doesn't need to be demeaned in the process?

Who will know he loves steamed broccoli, Brussels sprouts, summer fresh tomatoes, fresh corn, walnuts, ham and really rare thin sliced roast beef. Everyone who knows Ben well knows he loves cookies. How many people know he also loves soft pretzels with Grey Poupon mustard. He will accept Gulden's or French's, but Grey Poupon is his favorite.

Who will know that when he sees a fat black man, he will be terrified? His terror is real. He cannot shake these memories. He beats himself up because he thinks he should have been able to stop this hideous abuse; but he couldn't.

Sue Lehr

Who will know that a fat man treated him like garbage, making him clean his toilet and bathroom; taking him on long car trips instead of supporting Ben to do the things he wanted to do. Who will know, or care, when he is scared? Who will appreciate that he is vulnerable? He cannot speak easily. Everyone wants to control him. They try to restrain him. Who will understand that this is the worst form of abuse, it takes away all his dignity.

Who will understand that Ben is besieged with night terrors? Alone in his bedroom in the darkness, his night terrors become real and he cannot sleep. He starts beating himself up. Why? Who knows? But, he does and he screams and he cries, and he wants solace. Who will be there for him when these terrors overwhelm him? How will we support him? Who will be there when Bob and I are gone, dead? Who will be there?

Setting up trusts...

Rationally, we knew that one way we can assure that Ben is taken care of was to rewrite our wills and to consult a good attorney about what else we should do. When Bob was first diagnosed we read all the Alzheimer's literature on planning for the future, long term care options and legal protections. What we learned was not that different from what he had read regarding protecting children like Ben. We had just never thought that we would have to plan like this. Our attorney advised us to set up three trusts. The first was for Bob and his long-term care. We were candid with her. We were committed to providing care for Bob as long as he lived outside of any institution or residential care facility. He was so scared that he would have to go into one of these, but this plan assured us that he could stay where he wanted for as long as he lived. His retirement fund would provide the money to accomplish this.

We rewrote our wills, specifying that our estate would be divided into three equal portions so that each of our three children would inherit one third. Ben's portion will go into a trust - a supplemental needs trust - to take care of him. It will provide monies for those things he wants or would like to do, but cannot afford on his Social Security. Right now, he wants to go to the ocean on a camping trip. What a simple wish, but one which he could not afford on his current income. If later, after we die, he wants or needs something else, he can afford it; he can do it!

We also established a "Ben Lehr Residence Trust" which provides money for the taxes, maintenance and upkeep of his house. On the advice of our attorney, I took out a life insurance policy on myself and designated this trust as the beneficiary. If his house needs a new roof or repairs, whatever, there will be money to do that. Of course, it costs money, but I believe that fundamentally it is the right thing to do.

Beautiful Ben

So, who administers these? Right now, I am designated as the Trustee of each of these three trusts, with Penny as the successor Trustee. When I die, or if I die before Bob, Penny will become the Trustee of each. We have counseled her to invite our attorney to work with her along with my brother (a retired accountant and financial planner). It is a heavy burden to place on her, but one we know she will handle with love for her brother and us. We fundamentally believe that whatever decisions she makes will be right. She loves us and she loves Ben. We also know that legal protections are not enough. From our experiences we ask ourselves

"Who can we trust?". We had held on to the belief that if Ben was with his peers, non-disabled people, they would get to know him and become his natural supports. Through his experiences in school we saw this happen. We also recognized that Sherry and Penny, as Ben's sisters, were there for him, but as he approached adulthood, things naturally changed.

So who will be there when I am not?

Ben's life has moved on and so has he. He went through some rough times, really rough, but as more people got to know him he wasn't alone anymore. Today he has different friends who engage in his life in different ways. It no longer is important to me whether they are paid to be there or not. Ben doesn't care. He only wants people who respect him, give him the freedom to be who he is, don't try to control or restrain him, who see him as a mutual friend. Angelo, who works each day with Ben, is solid and caring. He enjoys being with Ben; finds him fun, funny, and sometimes frustrating. He has learned from Ben how to be supportive, but not intrusive; how to give guidance, but not direction or control; how to synchronize his rhythm with what Ben's flow of energy is that day; how to be there to work with Ben, not "on" Ben. Angelo is not governed by goals written as part of a behavior or work plan. He takes his lead from what Ben can do that day, what he can handle, how he feels, what he needs. He has learned to balance work in the shop with "outings" to buy supplies or for lunch or simply a walk in the park. He knows Ben and deeply cares about him as a person so he knows what Ben needs. Ben responds by giving Angelo hugs, smiles, and deep belly laughs. We would all be blessed to have one friend like Angelo.

Another friend is Brian, who is officially the Residential Coordinator for the agency (Onondaga Community Living, Inc.) that supports Ben. He chooses to spend time with Ben because they have become friends. When Ben's life was derailed by the actions of housemates and life experiences, Brian stepped in. He was there arranging for overnight support so that Ben could stay in his own home. He also decided to spend time each week with Ben, just hanging out, going places, getting to know each other. Brian believed that he needed to know Ben in order to support him well. Brian is a gentle, quiet, deeply caring man. He takes pride in what Ben is doing and he makes sure that Ben has what he needs to continue. He doesn't make a big deal about it, he just does it. He doesn't see this as his job. He genuinely likes Ben. He does see his job as finding the necessary supports so that Ben can live his life unencumbered, and so we are not bothered with forms, meetings, planning sessions, goal plans or any other bureaucratic garbage. He is quiet and humble, grateful to be given the freedom within the agency to do his job the way he thinks is right. Ben likes to be with Brian. There are other friends in Ben's life who contribute to his well-being and who he likes. We don't know them all, but we trust that Angelo, Brian, Pat (the agency executive director), Lauren (his service coordinator) and others will protect Ben, will value him such that they will never allow someone to hurt him again. Who will be there for Ben? These friends will!

There are other friends, not attached to any agency or service system. These are friends Ben has met most recently through Penny and Dee. They go camping together. They hang out with each other. They help each other and Ben is part of this. There are also friends that Ben has met through school, neighbors, others and us. These are people from all walks of life who look out for Ben, enjoy being with him, and accept him for who he is.

• •

A Story – The Lancaster Market

Recently the owner of the Lancaster Market, in Ben's old neighborhood, ran into him at a festival. He was so excited to see Ben. He told Ben how he finally had to sell the market and take a different job that would provide better benefits for his children. "I miss the store and the especially the customers, like you. "

"You know Ben, you were one of my best customers. Remember those cookies you loved so much? I just couldn't say 'no' to you, could I?" He grinned. "Hey, remember how you taught me to nuke those cinnamon buns in the microwave? People raved about how good they were warmed up like that. I think you are one of the smartest people I have ever met. I miss you, man."

• •

Because we have lived on the same dead-end street for over 30 years, neighbors often ask "How's Ben? We haven't seen him lately. Tell him we said

Beautiful Ben

hello." One neighbor makes sure that his swim raft is positioned just right so that Ben can swim down there whenever he wants. Bill will come out of his house or stop his lawn mowing and call out - "Hi Ben. How's the water?" Ben might not answer, in fact he often doesn't respond at all, but Bill knows Ben is listening. "Hey Ben, watch out for those big party boats this weekend. They might not be watching for you." Friends care about each other.

Does Ben have a girl friend? No. We wish he did. I think he wishes that too, but he just hasn't met anyone that he wants to date. He did have a girl friend once named Sarah. They enjoyed being together and her parents were very supportive, but distance and support became problematic. One day, when I asked Ben if he wanted to have a date with Sarah again, he typed NO. When I pushed him to explain why, he basically said that he had out grown her. He wasn't interested any longer.

Would I want Ben to date, marry, have sex? Yes, and yes and yes. He deserves the same right to these experiences as any other person. I think he would be so happy if he could find someone he could love. I have this romantic image of Ben and his "honey" holding hands, kissing, hugging and – yes - snuggling in bed together. Why not? Would I want them to have children? I obviously have an opinion, but this is not my decision. I trust Ben and his ability to make good decisions.

But, what of family?

Over the years, we have struggled to be sure that Penny and Sherry celebrated their brother and his unique accomplishments. We never wanted them to feel burdened by Ben. I don't think we succeeded, but we tried. We also wanted each of them to develop in their own way. When Sherry married Christian, a man she had met while studying in Germany, Christian asked Ben to be his best man. Ben's toast to the bride and groom, touched us all.

> BEFORE CHRISTIAN WAQS SHERRY - A REALLY
> GREAT PERSON. SHY TO OTHERS BUT VERY CARING
> UNDERSTANDING AND SWEET. BUT THERE ALWAYS
> SEEMED TO BE A PART THT WAS MISSINJG. THEN CAME
> CHRISTIAN. HE NOT ONLY HAS HE BEEN A HCXARING
> PERSON TO ME B8YUT HE HAS MAQDE MY SISTER
> HAPOPIOER. NOW THAT THEY ARE MARRIED IT MAKE
> ONE OF THE MOST CARINGB COUPLES I KNOW. I AM

VERY LUCKY TO BE CLOZSE TO THESE TWO PEOPLE.
CONGRADULATIONS AND I LKOVE YOU BOTH.

Penny - Our free spirit

That is who Penny is, a free spirit. Just like Sherry, "I am my own little person!" Penny has always set her own course. Each daughter is independent in her own way and I celebrate that. Penny has had a tough life, but she refuses to succumb to despair. She had her first child, Daniele, when she was 24. Brian, Daniele's father was killed in a freak snowmobile accident when she was eight months old. They came to live with us. Years later, she became involved with a truly great guy, Dee. They had a son, DeForest (named after his Dad), but life's troubles were only beginning for Penny and Dee. When DeForest was still an infant, their house was destroyed by an electrical fire. They moved home to live with us while they figured out what to do. Less than three weeks later, Dee was injured in an accident at work. He would live, but he would be disabled for the rest of his life. Penny and Dee lived with us for the next few years, while he recovered and they rebuilt their house. There were rough times, but we all made it because we stuck together. Ben was there too. He knew what was going on. He loves his sisters, and now he loves Dee, Daniele and DeForest, too. In a sense, they have become Ben's family. Penny and Dee's friends enjoy being with Ben also. They have become Ben's friends along with the other people who hang out with Ben. There are cookouts, bonfires, camping out under the trees on the far end of their 28 acres. And there is just "hanging out" time. It is like a family compound with Ben at the center.

A story –Life is good for Ben

"Hey Mom. You will never believe what is going on." I knew Penny was at Ben's house. She is there every Monday from about 1:30 on. Daniele and DeForest are at our house. Today, we did homework, made blueberry cupcakes and played. Penny usually calls to arrange when I should take them home, or if Dee would pick them up when he is finished work.

"Mom, this is so cool!" I could hear the excitement in her voice.

"Dee took Ben for a four-wheeler ride around his property. He loved it! But then, guess what? Dee asked Ben if he wanted to drive the four-wheeler. Can you believe it, Mom?

Ben handed Dee his soda and immediately got onto the driver's seat.

Beautiful Ben

Dee told him, 'Okay, Ben. Let's try it.' and Dee got on behind Ben."

My heart was racing waiting for Penny to say there had been an accident or something.

"Mom, Ben was driving really fast. Guess he got that from me." She was laughing. I wasn't.

"So anyway, Mom, Dee will pick up the kids around 5 - okay? We're going to take Ben home for dinner with us. Joe is coming later. We're going to play Foosball. Talk to you later. Love you, Mom." And she hung up.

"Hey Grams..." it was DeForest reminding me that we had been building an erector set high-rise building. We had been struggling with how to get the external elevator to work.

"Be right there." I looked at Daniele searching for iTunes on my computer.

She sensed me staring at her.

"Hi Grammi. This is cool." and she went back to her searching.

I walked slowly into the living room where DeForest was fitting together some support beams and windows for our "Blasier-Lehr Construction Business" office building.

"This is unbelievable." I thought about this as I slowly sat on the floor, next to DeForest.

"Ben is out driving a four-wheeler. Who would believe that he could do this?"

I went back to building with DeForest, but my mind was elsewhere. Driving a four-wheeler? Ben was not the passenger; he was driving.

A few days later Dee was telling me about this adventure. He smiled.

"And then, guess what happened? Ben came up behind me and hugged me and whispered 'friend' in my ear. Isn't that great?"

"You know, Sue, in the ten years I have known Ben, this is the happiest and most content I have ever see him." My eyes filled with tears.

"Yes, Dee, this is great!"

Where is Ben today?

He lives in his Cardiff house alone. Perhaps he finally got his wish of long ago – to live alone. Through Onondaga Community Living, he has the support he needs from people who care about him. He has meaningful work. He has friends who respect him, enjoy being with him. He has Penny and Dee and Daniele and DeForest who love him. Recently, they bought the house next door to Ben and, because there are over 28 acres of land, they have started an organic farm complete with chickens and ducks. They expect Ben to help with the chores, and he does.

"Isn't this great, Ben? We'll are living right next door. You can come over any time. There's a swimming pool too. You'll love that." The excitement in Penny's voice brought tears to my eyes. I could die tomorrow, I don't want to and have no plans for that, but I could and I would know that Ben will be fine, and he will be free.

So what have we learned?

Our life has been very complicated, very confusing, and very rich and good. I have loved our life, although I could have dealt with a little less strife. We have met some of the most incredible people because of our life with Ben. They have enriched us, and for that I will be grateful forever.

We have learned to listen to and respect what Ben has to say. We have learned not to let his disability, his autism, define who he is or what he can or cannot do. We have learned that asking for help is not a sign of weakness. People want to help. It makes us all feel good. We have learned to be more tolerant, vigilant, and thoughtful. People mean well, they just don't always do well. Most of all, we have learned to take one day at a time, not take ourselves too seriously, and to enjoy life and our family.

Beautiful Ben

Our first day with Ben — 1974

We thought all he needed was glasses

Ben-11, Sherry-17, Penny-13

Prom night — Ben and Alisha

Sherry and Christian's Wedding with best man – Ben, Penny, and the parents

Ben in his shop

I am a Perpendicular Angle

I am greater than right, greater than left. I am a perpendicular angle.

Clothes feel light because they are greater than the height of my body.

Great right angles shop, but they never have luck finding many buys.

Perpendicular angles never get to feel round, but they go happily up and down.

Ben Lehr

Ben wrote this poem as part of a competition for the Poetpouri, Jr. Comstock Writers Group Contest. It was published by the Syracuse City School District in 1992. As his family, we felt he was trying to tell people how complicated and multifaceted he was. We loved his reference to "they go happily up and down" – what a metaphor for his life.

JUST MY TYPE

BEN LEHR

REFLECTIONS

Throughout my education, behavioral problems get me really into trouble, in and out of class. I had no way actually to talk and let people know about my intelligence. Then I started facilitating and doors to classes and friendships opened. The teachers and students realized I had intelligence, humor, respect for others, and feelings, too. I go to T.V. production, math, art, gym, English, and lunch like all students. I type with my teachers Robin and Floris and lots of good friends. I facilitate conversations, homework, group discussions. I even did a monologue in my drama class.

I hope that facilitation can really reach out to open doors for people who don't have a voice. I think F.C. (facilitated communication) gives a different message. There are smart, good people inside autistic people. Try F.C. and the inner people can come out.

This was one of a series of articles Ben wrote for the Nottingham High School Newspaper. This particular article was published in June 1992. Having his photograph included in the series assured that people in the school would know who he was, what he faced daily, and how important it was/is to him for others to understand that people like him have so much to say and give.

NOT BEING ABLE TO SPEAK IS NOT THE SAME AS NOT HAVING ANYTHING TO SAY.

Written on a tee-shirt worn by Ben's teacher, Mrs. Palmer.

Acknowledgements and Reflections

As I wrote this, I sat in my Sunroom, as Ben called it. My computer glowed expectantly each night waiting for my wisdom and our stories. Through my windows I could see my gardens, my bird feeders, and most importantly, my lake. Virginia Wolff said we women writers must have a room of our own in which to write. I have that, but only now do I realize it is not the room, it is the people in the room with me that make it a rich place to be. My family, my friends, and the people who have made this book possible are there with me as I write. I could not do it alone.

I have told this story, Ben's story and ours', how I remembered it. Others may have perceived it differently. Let them tell their version, if they want. This is mine.

Our story is rife with anger at injustice, prejudice, racism, and the tension between inferiority and superiority. I do not apologize for my feelings or my anger. I find it incredibly hard to be gentle or gratuitous to those who have hurt Ben, but I also have to recognize that many of them did not understand what they were doing. They thought they were right, and I thought otherwise. In my personal moments of reflection, however, sometimes I wish things had been different.

When Ben was diagnosed with autism, we had no script of what our life would become. His autism was a conundrum that could not be explained in ways we understood. Maybe, in retrospect, this was a good thing. I know now, however, beyond any doubt, that we would not have survived so well if it were not for the people, the friends, who helped us along the way. How do I repay this debt of love and friendship? I can tell you their names, and I will, but you will probably not realize how important they were for our daily strength and survival.

For all the parents of children with disabilities, many of whom I have met over the years, I thank you for your courage and your resilience. Some, for me, deserve special attention. Martha Ziegler, Pat Amos, Barbara Cutler, Marilyn Wessels, Addy Comegys, Hillery Schneiderman, Betty Pendler, Sheree Burke, Magda Bayoumi – they are the freedom fighters of the parent movement, and there are so many more,

As we struggled and fought, we could not have done that without the support of so many truly good and committed people. Peter Knoblock, Ellen Barnes, Doug Biklen, Maurie Heins, Steve Taylor, Bob Bogdan, Gunnar Dybwad, Jan Nisbet, Alison Ford, Ann Donnellan, Jay Klein, Jeff Strully, Herb Lovett, Lou Brown, Steve Murphy, Burton Blatt, Bernice Schultz, Carol Berrigan, and so many others who put

Sue Lehr

their professional careers on the line because they believed in people like Ben. You gave us hope and affirmed our vision for Ben.

The front line of Ben's life was protected by teachers, administrators, professionals, and friends who were willing to listen to what he wanted to say, and who genuinely liked Ben and us. Valerie Fenwick, Chris Willis, Joe Marusa, Pat Floyd Echols. Mike "Doc" Marra, Michelle Dimon Borowski, Debbie Quick, Liz Altieri, Maureen Brophy, Pat Fratangelo, Brian Barney, Angelo Puccia and all of Ben's friends over the years - we salute you and honor your courage. Thank you for believing in us, for loving and respecting Ben, and most of all, for being his friend.

On a personal level, there are people whose support has sustained me in so many ways. Michael Kennedy, Cindy Sutton, Janet Duncan, Mike Berzonsky, and Emily and Russell Fudge – you are such true friends. I cannot thank you enough for what you have given me. I also must thank Allan Lallier, Ed Lancellotti, and Michelle Cryan, for giving me peace of mind as I struggled with this manuscript and my life. I hope you know how much it has meant.

And finally, to Sherry and Christian, and Penny and Dee – I love you. You, and your children, are my joy. You have been there all along. I lived this life with you and I could not have written these stories without you. And Ben and Bob – thank you for being who you are, and for allowing me to tell these stories.

Supplemental Reading

Biklen, D. (1990). Communication unbound: Autism and praxis. Harvard educational review, 60, pp. 291-314.

Biklen, D. (1992). Schooling without labels. Parents, educators, and inclusive education. Philadelphia: Temple University Press.

Biklen, D. (1993). Communication unbound. How facilitated communication is challenging traditional views of autism and ability/Disability. New York: Teachers College Press Columbia University.

Biklen, D. (2005). Autism and the might of the person alone. New York: New York University Press.

Biklen, D. & Cardinal, D.N. (1997). Contested words – Contested science. Unraveling the facilitated communication controversy. New York: Teachers College, Columbia University.

Berube, M. (1996). Life as we know it. A father, a family, and an exceptional child. New York: Vintage Books – A Division of Random House, Inc.

Harry B. (2008). Melanie: Bird with a broken wing. Xlibris Corporation.

Lovett, H. (1996). Learning to listen –Positive approaches and people with difficult behavior. Baltimore, MD: Paul H. Brookes Publishing Co.

National Research Council (2001). Educating children with autism. Washington, DC:National Academy Press.

Savarese, R. J. (2007). Reasonable People – a memoir of autism & adoption. New York: Other Press.

Shapiro, J. P. (1993). No pity. People with disabilities forging a new civil rights movement. New York: Times Books Random House.

Shumaker, L. (2008). A regular guy – Growing up with autism. Lafayette, CA: Landscape Press.

Woolf, V. (1929). A room of one's own. Orlando, FL: Harcourt, Inc.

Websites

www.autcom.org – Autism National Committee – Dedicated to social justice for all citizens with autism.

www.ASA.org – Autism Society of America – Improving the lives of all affected by autism

www.bbl.syr.edu – Burton Blatt Institute at Syracuse University

www.CHP.edu – Center on Human Policy Law and Disability Studies at Syracuse University

www.InclusionInstitutes.org – Facilitated Communication Institute and others

www.Jowonio.org – a non-profit school for young children with a wide range of abilities

www.TASH.org – Equity, opportunity and inclusions for people with disabilities

www.Wrightslaw.org – A leading website about special education law and advocacy

Each of these sites have links to other informative sites.

Ariminta Books

Ariminta Books is dedicated to enabling people with disabilities and their families to tell their own stories as they have lived them. The goal is to develop a better understanding of how their disabilities impact individuals and their families, one story at time. Through their words, experiences, stories, and thoughts, each book reveals what life is like day in and day out for one person or one family.